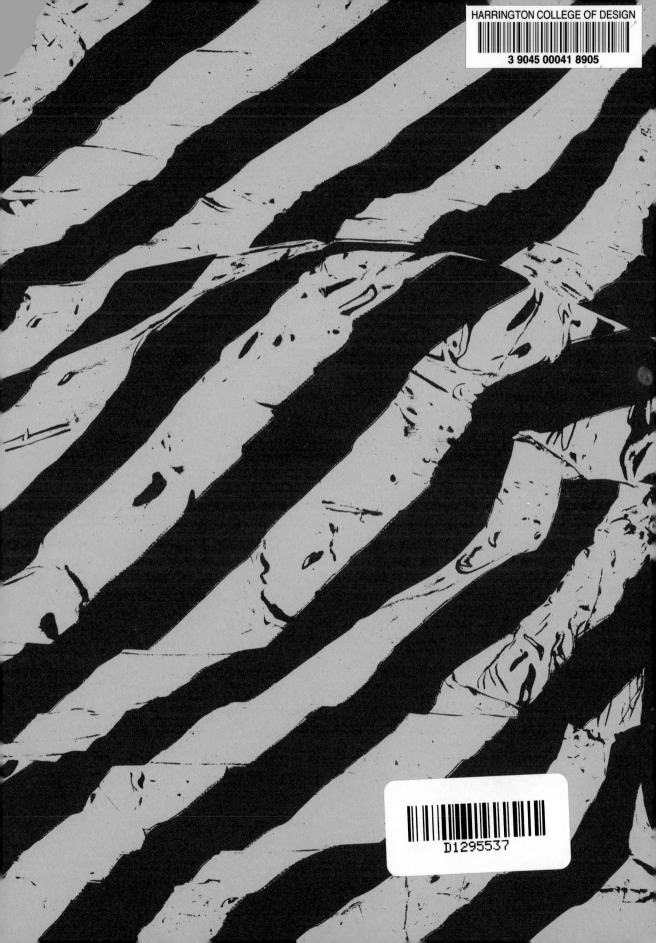

Construction Site
Metamorphoses in the City
Marie Antoinette Glaser (ed.)

Lars Müller Publishers

ETH
Eidgenössische Technische Hochschule Zürich
Swiss Federal Institute of Technology Zurich

Department Architecture
ETH Wohnforum / ETH Centre for Cultural Studies in Architecture

CONTENTS

PREFACE

Construction Site. Metamorphoses in the City

Life is a Construction Site – it is perhaps not surprising that this was the title given to one of Germany's most successful films in the 1990s. Indeed, it seems that as a metaphor for the patchwork of contemporary ways of life, the construction site is experiencing something of a boom. In its capacity for transformation it has become a symbol of the innate character of our post-modern society. The phenomenon of the construction site is present in our everyday experience and yet remains fenced off, concealed. It is time to investigate the construction site in all its dimensions...

On the idea for this book

Most publications in the field of architecture and construction tend to concentrate on the finished building and the work of individual, outstanding architects. By contrast, public attention is rarely focused on the complex process of construction and the people involved in it, or on the planning and logistics of structural engineering, although they are all essential elements of every outstanding building. All too often, it is the problems of noise, dust and traffic that tend to dominate the public perception of the construction site. And yet the construction site is much more than this. It constitutes an remarkable locus within the urban landscape, a microcosm that functions under a high level of pressure in terms of time and cost. The construction site is a harsh reality and at the same time an exciting and well-organized enterprise that requires the coordination of material, people, machines and media.

Construction Site. Metamorphoses in the City uses an interdisciplinary perspective to look at and into the construction site as a complex and fascinating workspace. The book aims to present the phenomenon of the construction site both textually and pictorially, in a way that combines a general overview with specialist knowledge. It is thus intended as an exciting source of information and inspiration for interested laypeople, city dwellers and urban *flâneurs* as well as a fund of new and unfamiliar perspectives for building professionals. For both groups of readers it is designed to present the construction site as a place that invites exploration. By exploring the construction site as a microcosm, the authors have developed a multilayered image of the practical realities as well as the symbolic and aesthetic dimension of the construction site within our culture.

Marie Antoinette Glaser

CHAP. 01

THE CON- STRUCTION SITE

HISTORY AND PRESENT OF A FASCINATION

Marie Antoinette Glaser

Who of us has not felt the tug of curiosity as we walked past the hoarding around a construction site? And who of us has managed to resist stopping at the first gap we come across and peeking through to see what purpose the ear-splitting din of construction machinery is actually serving? Usually we see groups of workers, some laboring away at dizzying heights, with an array of materials, machinery and hand tools. Sometimes we even catch a glimpse of the architects in conversation with site managers and visiting investors. Of late we have even been able to satisfy our curiosity by taking part in public construction-site tours, attending construction sites lunches with machinery demonstrations, or visiting on-site information centers and viewing terraces. Spyholes and platforms invite us, the outsiders, to take in the spectacle of the construction site.

Enjoyment and Exasperation
However, what we do not see here are the complex, intermeshed processes that constitute the actual workings of a construction site. The roaming, untrained eye is not capable of comprehending the immense technical and logistical effort required for the construction of new buildings. While

for planners, architects, engineers and construction experts, the construction site as microcosm is a self-evident element of the context in which they practice their professions daily, most of us city dwellers, whether as neighbors, passers-by or tourists, remain strictly laypeople, at times astounded, at times annoyed—and always at a safe distance. As part of our everyday lives, the construction site as annoyance means noise, dirt, dust, blocked footpaths and rerouted streets. However, as a "black box" that is passed every-day, the construction site awakens many people's interest. Older people are drawn to it as a kind of cinematic event. Children stand in front of it in awe. Artists, flâneurs and designers have long found the construction site to be a source of inspiration within the smoothly functioning urban space. It is an open promise of what is to come. But what is it that constitutes its fascination and allure for so many different groups of people?

A World of Contrasts

The allure of the construction site is based not so much on the anticipation of the completed building, which can in any case be viewed in computer simulations, as on its uniqueness as a space. The breach in what is otherwise a systematically constructed cityscape, its provisional character and perpetual movement hold the promise of excitement and discovery. The con-struction site draws our interest because it appears composed of contrasts. While experts emphasize the controlled order of the activities and the space as the highest priority of the construction process and the importance of meticulous logistical planning at every stage, the passing observer sees a confusion of different types of work going on that evokes a sense of the raw and unfinished, of constant change. Every stroke of the digger is a violent intervention in the surface of the city, and every excavation pit reveals the rawness beneath the pulsating urbanity around it, sometimes down to the brown, up-welling water table. An apparently chaotic conglomeration of excavated earth, machines, cables and flapping tarps reinforce the impression of unpredictability. And indeed, every construction site contains real dangers for those who are unfamiliar with it.

Moreover, the building site is unexplored territory, temporary terrain vague, which, as long as the building has not been inaugurated, con-tinues to exist within the urban public space without any economic use or function. It is unreconnoitered terrain, since unauthorized entry is subject to legal penalty. And yet the process of construction always takes place in public view. Construction sites publicly exhibit work. They are temporarily erected production facilities of the building trade and the construction industry in the midst of public space. In contrast to the workshops and assembly shops in other industries, they and the technical processes going on within them are almost completely visible and thus assessable for everyone. For this reason, they offer themselves as individual objects of study and attract acclaim or critical comments, often from ingenuous laypeople. We might surmise that the publicly visible (physical) work being performed in this context exerts a particular fascination in a time when work has become a rarified commodity for so many and for the most part takes place on computer monitors and in air-conditioned meeting rooms. Perhaps in the 21st century we can no longer speak of the cult of the worker that gained such currency in the 1920s and subsequent decades, but must instead refer to the „cult of work" in a post-Fordian, postmodern and digitalized Western society that is developing a romanticized yearning for the reality of manual work.

The Construction Site as an Emblem of its Time
In recent years the building site has become the symbol of a society aspiring to progress and growth. As the emblem of an epoch it has undergone a transformation, from bone-breaking building work to highly complex projects which can only be carried out in an estimated time using sophisticated logistics, constant quality control and professional communication with the surroundings (Franz Pröfener, "Flirting with disaster. Zur Symbolgegenwart der 'Baustelle',"" Zeitzeichen Baustelle, ed. F. Pröfener (Frankfurt / New York, 1998), pp. 6-47). The construction site would seem to mirror the disposition of our postmodern society. As an image it has assumed a firm place in our collective consciousness. And it is this image that we encounter in our everyday urban lives and in our everyday use of the media. On the Internet, live webcams offer us a view of the progress of spectacular and less spectacular building projects. In the media, construction sites are not only used as a vehicle for present avant-garde fashions; the building site has also been taken up as a theme by companies, banks and Swiss scholars. The Swiss daily press increasingly uses the construction site in its headlines. In 2005 the NZZ am Sonntag featured the titles "Life Is a Construction Site" and "Construction Site Switzerland" in the space of only three pages. As a metaphor of contemporary social change, the building site is experiencing something of a boom. It appears as a symbol of upheaval within permanence and can thus be read allegorically as an increasing affirmation of transformation processes, flexibility and the mobility of life and work in our society.

A further important observation, only seldom do we see women there. The construction site remains one of the few male professional domains, along with drilling platforms in the North Sea and the Foreign Legion. It is only slowly that women are encroaching on the territory of laborers, site

managers, engineers, architects, planners, investors and project developers. However, this should change in the future.

The Last Utopia?

Building numbers among the paradigmatic activities in our culture (The concept of paradigmatic activity is drawn from the work of the sociologist Klaus Türk. See Klaus Türk, Bilder der Arbeit. Eine ikonografische Anthologie, (Wiesbaden, 2000), especially pp. 82-88). Building marks the distinction between nature and culture. Since the Middle Ages, building as constructive—that is, founding—work has been deployed as an allegory for the mastery of natural forces by human beings and their capacity to detach themselves from an existence as mere natural entities. → ILL.01.01

At the same time, the symbolic content of building primarily inheres in the achievements of construction and the finished product rather than in the activity of building itself. It is still the case that this organizational and technical achievement is generally attributed to the architect, the engineer or perhaps the property developer, but never to those who have actually performed the work. In the 20th century the construction site also became the symbol of socialist modernity in that it gave visual expression to construction, productivity and (for the first time) the labor of the worker, progress,

ILL.01.01
The Tower of Babel (Vienna Version)
Pieter Brueghel the Elder, 1563

13

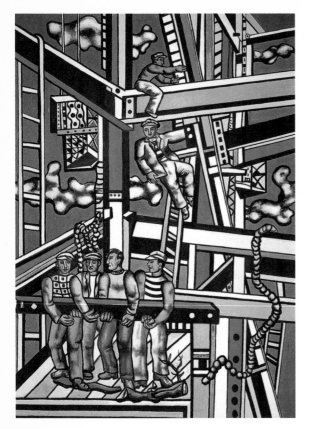

ILL.01.03
Construction Workers on a High Rise, Guangzhou, 1996

ILL.01.02
Fernand Léger, Les Constructeurs, 1950

prosperity, technical mastery of space and (male) engineering skills. → **ILL.01.02**
This pathos of the construction site was still evident at the inauguration
of Berlin's Potsdamer Platz when, in October 1996, 19 building cranes "danced"
to Beethoven's "Ode to Joy" conducted by Daniel Barenboim.

The large-scale building site promises growth, prosperity and feasibility
by means of organization and the considered deployment of materials and
people. Throughout history it has been primarily streets and bridges that have
served to represent the might and grandeur of those in power. Today's
vast city and dam construction projects in China can also be read as a contemporary symbol of the mastery of space, time and human beings by the
ruling nomenklatura, as can the construction projects launched under the rule
of National Socialism in Germany and the megalomaniacal building schemes
characteristic of totalitarian states in general. They were and are intended as

an expression of absolute power of the rulers. The aura of the great construction sites of pyramids, cathedrals and palaces—which retained a presence as construction sites for decades and even centuries—was based on the superhuman dimensions and the sacred character of the buildings. They were challenges that were taken on despite exceeding the humanly possible. In the secularized society of modernity, large-scale building projects no longer represent a link between the human and the divine, in the way the Tower of Babel was intended to link the earth with the highest on high. And yet a sacred metaphor still adheres to them. The construction site is a secular symbol of the modern world. It promises the certainty of conquering space with one's own power and ability. The idea of the sheer technical possibilities involved still evokes a kind of dizzying grandeur.

The construction site embodies dynamism, process and constant change; it is a state of suspense full of expectation, the promise of the new and a locus of transition amidst the otherwise regulated everyday urban environment. As a state of pre-completion and dynamism it also becomes symbolic of all productive processes; we speak of the writing desk as construction site, of literature as a construction site, of reunification as a construction site, of Switzerland as a construction site or of Europe as a construction site. Does the construction site as a promise of possibility and growth perhaps even represent one of the last utopias of our postmodern society? An utopia that continues to exert a power from within a modernity whose failure we have long recognized in terms of the price it demands, i.e., environmental destruction, resource scarcity and unjust social distribution? → ILL.01.03

The Construction Site as Disruptive Factor
The construction site is a constant feature of our everyday urban experience. It is part of the symbolic landscape of the modern city, as Alfred Döblin's protagonist Franz Biberkopf experiences in the Berlin of the 1920s. On his foray through Berlin following his release from prison, Biberkopf passes several building sites: the streets on Rosenthaler Platz are being torn up, the subway is being built, and in Münzstrasse hoarding obscures the view. Pedestrians gather to catch a glimpse of what is going on below.

For a short time (compared with the subsequent life of the finished building), the construction site knocks a hole in the series of smooth facades—and "disrupts" the familiar cityscape. The sudden strangeness alters our habitual perception and opens up new perspectives: "It is only construction sites, elements of disruption, that create an open place, that allow the space to emerge," writes Friedrich Achleitner (Friedrich Achleitner, "Zur Wahrnehmung altstädtischer Räume. Das touristische Paradoxon," in Wiener Architektur: zwischen typologischen Fatalismus und semantischem Schlamassel (Vienna/Cologne/Weimar, 1996), p. 209.). And yet, as embodiments of the urban, they are substantial attributes of this space. With its noise, dust, heat, welding flames and steam, the construction process embodies, as it were, the factory of the street.

At this point we perhaps need to differentiate more precisely between the type of construction site involved in road works and the type associated with structural building projects. Whereas the former has now become a daily annoyance that most people encounter on their way to work or on vacation trips, the latter often tends to evoke a sense of wonder as we watch the new building rising into the skyline. In recent years road works have become such a frequent hindrance in our lives that it is hard to conceive of anyone serving coffee and cake to laborers working on nearby road projects—as could still be observed, for example, 20 years ago in Zurich. Nowadays, living near the site of such road works is more likely to result in stress and annoyance and can even be a reason for demanding a rent reduction. And if one understands the street in Walter Benjamin's sense as a "home of the collective," then it would seem that every construction site in the city constitutes a disturbance to our everyday domesticity. For pedestrians and residents, they mean noise, dirt and dust—usually over a period of months. We often pass them holding our breath with our eyes averted, hoping that this apparition will soon be exorcised.

"The beauty of the beast"

Nevertheless, a certain fascination remains as we pass each day the site of a newly emerging building. Each time, we spot a new change, some progress in the development of the building shell. The daily search for the latest developments becomes a game we engage in on what is other-wise the same monotonous route to work. Somehow the process of emergence seems more exciting for us than the later result; as soon as the building is completed, the surfaces sealed and the cranes disassembled, the end result, paradoxically, is no longer perceived—because its appearance no longer changes and becomes yet another habitual sensation for the eye.

During construction, on the other hand, new, unreproducible views in fleeting moments of sudden beauty constantly emerge. In such moments, a scaffolding structure or a roof beam texture becomes a filigree geometric pattern. The steel frame construction of a high-rise building with its static calmness has a majestic effect within the streetscape. Our fascination is based on the constructional thinking behind the viewed object. As Mies van der Rohe writes, "It is only while under construction that skyscrapers reveal the audacious, constructional thinking that informs them; the impression created by the towering steel frame is overwhelming. Cladding the facades completely destroys this impression, eliminates the constructional thought, the foundation of the artistic composition." (Mies van der Rohe, "Hochhäuser," Frühlicht I (1922), tome 4; cited in Fritz Neumeyer, Mies van der Rohe. Das kunstlose Wort: Gedanken zur Baukunst (Berlin, 1986), p. 298.)

The Eroticism of the Construction Site?

The construction site projects into public space. It is a spectacle and a sensation for the inhabitants of the modern metropolis. Day and night it draws the gaze of passers-by for it does not move. The illumination of the large-scale construction site at night and the flames of the welding torches coalesce into a staged architecture of light that is all the more awe-inspiring due to its ephemeral character. The manifold disguises assumed by the construction event attract the eye. Can we speak here of an eroticism of the construction site? If so, then it is one based on the interplay between exposure and concealment, which feeds the everyday voyeurism of the urban dweller. In this context, fences, scaffolding, tarpaulins, fabric and netting work to regulate perception by obscuring the view while also drawing attention by means of striking colors and expansive surfaces. In some cases, when washed-out cloth and waving nets, which are actually there to keep dust and rain off the structure for a brief time, evoke their own rough charm, the effect is completely unintended. The openings and holes that are created then allow for a clandestine view into the interior of the construction site. → ILL.01.04

Building firms have long been aware that construction sites function as business cards. How they look can be decisive in attracting further commissions and public support or rejection. The design of large urban construction sites such as Potsdamer Platz in Berlin and Ground Zero in New York are meticulously monitored by public relations experts. The design and communication concept of a construction site can make a significant contribution to its acceptance by affected parties and the public at large—skillful design and events work to focus interest and direct the public eye to particular visually attractive sections in order to diminish the memory of unpleasant phases of dirt and noise.

Documents of the Unfinished

As a rule it is only completed structures that are found in the archive of public memory. The exciting process of their emergence is normally not stored over the longer term. Thus it is only pictures like those by Lewis Wickes Hine that enable us to visualize the construction of the Empire State Building, or the different stages involved in the construction of the Eiffel Tower or the

ILL.01.05
Construction workers at the Empire State Building, Lewis W. Hine, New York, 1930

ILL.01.04
Tarpaulins on scaffolding, Barcelona

Cologne Cathedral. → **ILL.01.05** Anonymous photographs take by construction workers provide us with additional information concerning historical practices and organizational approaches within the building industry. Professional architectural photography for contemporary magazines and journals tends to feature aesthetically perfect, freshly completed and still unused surfaces. The apparently chaotic construction building process that lies behind them, which is characterized by piles of diverse building materials, protruding wiring and cables stretching up into the air, is seldom photographed except as a record of deficiency and failure. One exception is that of particularly spectacular buildings, which are photographed from the first day of construction onwards. It is not uncommon for nearby residents and tourists to document the progress of such projects. What is it that drives them? Are they seeking to retain a vivid memory of this urban gap? Are their snapshots driven by the need to bear witness amidst the ever more rapid pace of urban development? Are they an amateurish attempt to participate in an urban dynamic in the global centers of late capitalist society? Or, conversely, are they rather an attempt to preserve a moment that can never be repeated?

Today the building site numbers among the day-to-day experiences that are unavoidably encountered in the urban space. From afar, the construction site of a major building, as a locus of change and permanent transition, signals a future orientation. Experienced up close, it usually constitutes a nerve-wracking nuisance. However, the construction site has long been more than merely a visible disruption in the urban space. It has become a place of fascination and a contemporary cultural phenomenon, shaped by the live worlds around it. This book is thus designed not only to survey the past, present and future of the building site from different standpoints, but also to provide an impulse for reflection on the present and future disposition of our society.

CHAP. 02

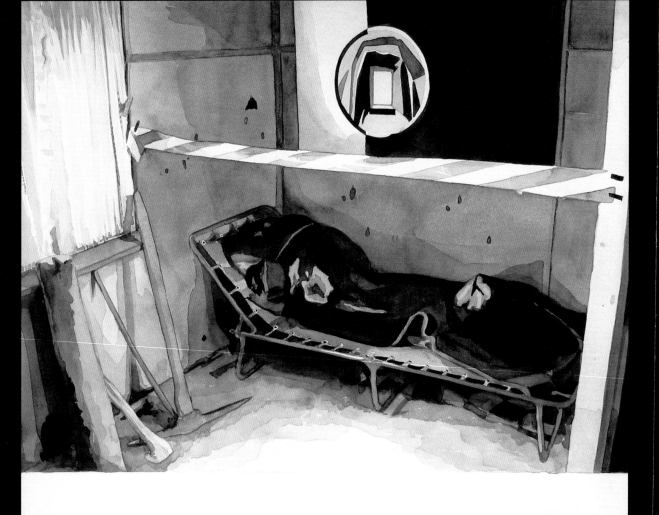

Jana Gunstheimer
Über F./F. lebt beengt, 2006
water color on paper, 32,7 x 38 cm

THE DREAM OF FLYING

THE PROSPECTS FOR DIGITAL PLANNING AND CONSTRUCTION PROCESSES

Sacha Menz

When in 1836 Michael Thonet invented the process of bending wood for furniture construction in the German town of Boppard—a process he later developed further in Vienna—he could not have predicted the economic success his idea would have. By 1930 he and his descendents, working under the name of 'Thonet Brothers,' had produced and sold 50 million copies of the world-renowned No. 14 bentwood chair. It was a technological breakthrough. What had previously been individually handcrafted products could now be made available to the broad mass of the population. → ILL.02.01

Industrial mass production has now become established over a vast range of areas. The demand in world markets for high-quality industrially manufactured products is increasing constantly, and along with short-term availability and large quantities there are a number of other prominent demand criteria. One of the most fundamental of these is the individualization of the mass product. In highly developed and organized societies, one expression of the individual's desire to distinguish him or herself from the great mass of the population can be seen in the demand for individualized products. Price plays a decisive role here. Manufacturers able to offer individualized mass products at the same or lower production costs will be able to assert themselves in the market of the future. The development of the Internet is playing an important role in this respect—on the one hand due to the almost unlimited access it provides to consumers, and on the other due to its capacity to create the simultaneous interlinking of development and production. A side effect is that habits on the demand and the supply side can be easily comprehended using opinion polls and statistics—information which in turn is used for the further development of products. Anyone who uses a customer-points card provided by department store chains or orders products over the Internet should be aware that their purchasing habits are being stored in a database and may be used to improve performance and for further product development by the service providers concerned.

The development of the building industry can hardly be compared with the extraordinary pace of change in the field of industrial mass production. The processes described above have been applied only rudimentarily or not at all on the construction site. Construction, construction sites and their associated logistics are still traditionally organized for the most part and can still be seen as typical examples of the manual trades. For example, in bricklaying, bricks and mortar are still used according to traditional methods on construction sites. And in Asia, scaffolding is still predominantly constructed using traditional bamboo technology. → ILL.02.02

ILL.02.02
Construction site in Shanghai with scaffolding
made of bamboo

ILL.02.01
Michael Thonet, Bentwood Chair No.14,
Vienna, 1859–1930

In the coming years and decades, industrial planning and production processes will have to adapt to strong pricing and demand pressures. The production processes used in the highly developed automobile and aviation industries are already working with digital technology. The following two examples are indicative of the current state of development in this regard. When purchasing a car, the customer visits the Internet pages of the selected manufacturer and logs into the system via a car configurator. The virtual assembly of the customer's desired vehicle commences on the computer screen, irrespective of location and free of any obligation. Every production step is documented online; surfaces and fittings are shown, as well as changes in price and delivery times based on specific customer preferences that deviate from the basic model. In theory, such a system allows for 10^{32} variations on the BMW 3 Series. Since the process of configuration can take up several pleasurable hours, customers have the option of "parking" their vehicle in a virtual garage, i.e., of storing their data in order to be able to work on it at a later time. → ILL.02.03

Once customers have configured their dream car, they can take it for a test drive at a dealership in their region. If requested, a leasing company of the car manufacturer can offer an installment plan for payment. Customers can alter different details of their vehicles up to a few days prior to the commencement of manufacture, which is completed in ten to 15 hours. Such a system requires a clearly structured and organized component-supply industry. The car producer's assembly factory assembles module components that are ordered and delivered at short notice. A company such as BMW typically limits itself to the production of motors, doors and a number of other components. While automobile production is one of the more advanced areas in this regard, analogous restructuring of developmental and production processes can also be seen in other industries. The aim is to achieve more rapid and precise delivery, lower cost products and a better integration of the individual customer's preferences.

The construction of aircraft at different production centers would also not be possible without the application of such procedures. The European Airbus Industries is a good example in this regard. A jet consists of some 3.5 million individual parts, which are manufactured by more than 6000 suppliers throughout the world. The printed interior paneling of the cabins, for example, is ordered online and custom-made by a family-owned firm near Cleveland, Ohio in the USA, according to the purchasing airline's preferences. A range of factories in Germany, France, Great Britain and Spain pre-assemble individual parts into so-called fractions, which are then integrated in the final assembly in Toulouse. → ILL.02.04

ILL.02.03
Car Configurator, BMW 3 Series Touring, www.bmw.ch

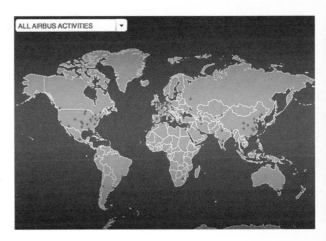

ILL.02.04
"All Airbus Activities", www.airbus.com
How does the building industry figure in all this? What will
the construction sites of tomorrow look like?

ILL.02.05
Monte Rosa Hütte, Guest room, Wallis 2006

A research project at ETH Zurich (the Swiss Federal Institute of Technology
Zurich) is currently looking into the digitalized production of complete,
three-dimensional building modules. The technology involved will make it possible to design and develop the wooden structure of the Swiss Alpine Club's
new Monte Rosa hut, the structure's cladding and three-dimensional modules of
its rooms on a computer screen. This process will also involve consultation
with the firms involved regardingthe building's architectural coherence, stability,
accessibility, producibility and price. The process is aimed at the direct
application of the specified structural elements and represents a clear departure
from the traditional, still common approach based on separate planning,
tendering, contracting and implementation steps. → **ILL.02.05**

Will the dream of flying in the sense of a digital-process revolution on
building sites become a reality? Will the building sites of the future be

ILL.02.06
La costruzione di un palazzo, Piero di Cosimo, 1515–1520

computer-controlled assembly shops in which buildings are produced day and night, protected from weather, noise, dust and unions? Will we soon be able to order our own home on a computer screen without the involvement of an architect, in the same way the car industry is already enabling us to order a car?

Looking back to the Renaissance may shed some light on the cautious development of ostensibly innovative planning and construction processes in the building industry. Up until Leon Battista Alberti formulated his new theses on architecture around 1452, the tasks of the architect were basically divided into three roles. He was the *sapiens architectus*, who was responsible for the design; the *magister operis*, the master builder; and the *magister lapidum*, which corresponded to the site foreman of modern parlance. This definition corresponds to what we know from the books of the large German cathedral building workshops of the time, the *Dombauhütten*. The so-called *fabricae ecclesiae* involved teams of master builders, journeymen, apprentices and unskilled laborers. The intellectual upheaval of the Renaissance not only liberated the sciences but also exerted an effect on the construction site, particularly on the way construction was planned and carried out.

The panel *La costruzione di un palazzo* by Piero di Cosimo was completed around 1520. → ILL.02.06 The picture uses a kind of time-lapse method to illustrate the idea of a construction site and its protagonists, from the planners to the craftsmen and specialists involved in the building process. The panoramic format enables the artist to express the idea of holism. At the same time, the foundation of knowledge and work referred to by Alberti in his enumeration of the different disciplines found on the building site is represented here pictorially by the groups of figures scattered across the entire painting. The two architects of the building project, the brothers Giuliano and Antonio da Sangallo, stand neither in the picture's foreground nor in its axial center, but are seen with their backs turned to the viewer. Sitting on two horses, socially elevated, the two protagonists responsible for the architectural concept are turned to face the fundamental subject of the panel, the palazzo, which is partly finished and partly still under construction. The painting makes clear the natural quality, availability and suitability of the selection of materials. Workers haul wood from forests, stone from mountain quarries and sand from distant lakes or rivers. The building material, which is cut to size or already of suitable dimensions, is stacked in an orderly pile. The depiction makes clear the necessary ability and intelligence of the planners and architects, which are symbolized in the precise selection of the location and the correct proportions and stability of the building. And lastly, there is the craftsman, *artigiano* in Italian, the real artist, who does the work and is responsible for implementing the prescribed idea. Through the formative character of the material, he lends the whole its form and, in an ingenious transformation, translates the tangible material into artistic and human order. Carpenters and masons represent the human tools of planners and architects, whose craft and technologies they are intimately acquainted with. From planning and execution to functional end product, the building process is presented in this picture as a holistic act, which unifies science, technology, handcraft and artistic and social activities. And in the midst of all this, turned towards the object—creating, organizing and communicating—stands the architect.

In terms of conception and organization, the construction sites of today bear more than a passing resemblance to the depiction by Piero di Cosimo. There is no doubt that over the course of time, different work processes have been tightened up and optimized with the help of new technologies. On the other hand, shovels, picks, trowels and hammers as well as other archaic tools are still being widely used on constructions sites.

Individualized mass production is not a temporary fashion but a reflection of the social and industrial development of our time, and it will inevitably find its way into all industries, including the construction industry. However, industrial mass production has never been able to establish itself on the construction site to the same degree as it has in the car industry. In the construction sector, such mass production is still limited to prefabricated building components, elements and modules, which represent the peak of industrialization within the building industry. Precast concrete segments have become standard on construction sites and can be found in catalogs on the Internet. Prefabricated three-dimensional modules, for instance for bathrooms and kitchens, have established themselves in the market to a limited degree within a certain price and quality range. However, when producing pre-fabricated components building suppliers still tend to rely on conventional manufacturing methods. For example, prefabricated brickwork, although produced in controlled climatic conditions, is still laid by hand. → **ILL.02.07**

Construction essentially remains a manual craft, and only certain aspects of it have been subject to the highest levels of industrial production. However, the application of new technologies based on digitally interlinked processes could change this. The fundamental difference between automobile production and construction has to do with the possibilities of continuous production under calculable and controllable conditions. All the factors influencing industrial production originate from people and hence can be steered by them. The automobile is a closed system in the sense that as a receptacle on wheels it is clearly delineated from its surroundings. Any incalculable factors that could constitute an obstacle for mass production are associated not with the factory but with the street. Given a clear separation between closed and open systems, car production can be increasingly controlled and perfected. → **ILL.02.08**

A building also exhibits a clear system boundary, in terms of its link with a particular location, its foundations and its connection to media. However, the unpredictability of the building ground and the problems inherent in under-ground engineering make prefabrication in this area impossible. Manu-facturing buildings using modern industrial processes requires in the first place a platform, whose function is equivalent to that of the street in car production. Only then will it be possible, under controllable conditions, to construct a complete building using industrial methods and a digitalized work process that runs from planning to production. The idea of a platform is not new. The avant-garde movement of the 1960s was already aware of this problem and radicalized it in two directions. While Superstudio envisaged a gigantic platform suitable for all needs, which made any additional structure redundant, Archigram proposed the "Plug-in City" and the "Walking City," which were not tied to a particular location and used the ground as a platform. → **ILL.02.09**

It is only pressure in terms of price and deadlines that will drive forward and hone automated production. Labor markets such as China and India, where real wages are far below those in the Western world, will be able to take their time in this respect. And for this reason it is countries such as Japan and Switzerland that have an interest in the development of automated systems for construction sites. These entail above all mobile robotic systems for wall assembly and for reinforcement, distribution and compaction in concrete construction. → **ILL.02.10**

Felix Schramm

Der Bau, 2005
Installationview,
Galerie ausstellungsraum25, Zurich

Felix Schramm

Der Bau, 2005
Installationview,
Galerie ausstellungsraum25, Zurich

ILL.02.07
Prefabricated concrete columns,
Angelo Mangiarotti, Milan 1987

ILL.02.08
Mobile house being towed by a truck, USA

EACH WALKING UNIT HOUSES NOT ONLY A KEY
ELEMENT OF THE CAPITAL , BUT ALSO A LARGE
POPULATION OF WORLD TRAVELLER-WORKERS.

A WALKING CITY

ILL.02.09
Walking Cities, Ron Herron, Archigram, London 1964

ILL.02.10
Construction robot ROCCO

Such developments are proceeding only slowly. Research in the robotics field is clearly showing that for the time being researchers need to focus their efforts on more promising areas such as medicine and artificial intelligence. The firms that are dealing most intensively with these kinds of issues at present are the prefabricated house manufacturers. And it is not surprising that it is this sector that has produced the first house configurators, which allow clients to design their own dream house on a computer screen.

The role of the configurator here is above all that of a tool; its secondary function is as an interface between clients and producers, and in this sense it assumes the role of the retailer. Unlike in the consumer goods industry, where the retailer has always played a role, in the building industry this function, where it has existed at all, has until now been assumed by the architect. The deployment of the house configurator thus amounts in one sense to a decrease in the architect's field of competence. The work that architects have until today invested in mediating and adapting their designs must now be integrated into the configurator so that it becomes accessible to everyone. The fact that the work of design thereby becomes reproducible for everyone represents a completely new element for the field of architecture. As a consequence, adaptable and parameterized design concepts are becoming architects' real assets, and they will become increasingly inter- rested in protecting their rights through patents.

This development is characteristic of a society in which the centralization and codification of knowledge plays a predominant role. However, the question of the extent to which spatial concepts represent a technical invention and can thus be patented will only be answered in the concrete legal context. Regardless of what the outcome is, an alternative approach to licensing, as proposed by the open source movement in the software industry, is also conceivable and even desirable. As yet it is not clear what route architecture will take. However, what is clear is that the old system will not lose its validity but will instead continue to exist parallel to the new one.

Seen from this perspective, the realization of the dream of flying in the construction industry and on the construction site of the future still needs time. After all, it was not until 32 years after Otto Lilienthal's first historic flights in 1895 that Charles Lindbergh flew across the Atlantic.

CHAP. 03

THE CON- STRUCTION SITE AND THE ARCHITECT

ARCHITECTURE AS IDEA AND REALISATION

An Interview with: Dietmar Eberle (Architect Baumschlager & Eberle, Lochau, Austria)
Questions: Peter Kaufmann (Architect)

You have—together with your clients—worked on building sites yourself. What is it about the way you see yourself as an academic that motivated you to do manual construction work?

I don't see any essential difference either in terms of the quality of work or the way it's understood and appreciated. So doing manual work on a construction site doesn't conflict with the image I have of myself at all; for me, it's something self-evident that has to do with my background and my very regionally anchored understanding of life. After completing my studies I was fairly skeptical towards academics. I regarded people who worked with their hands as somehow more connected with the future, as more intelligent and more valuable for our society than academics. This view was also based on the gulf between my academic training as an architect and the reality of construction in the everyday world. For me, working as a manual laborer meant clearly defining myself outside the academic understanding of architecture. Of course, such a stance can also be analyzed on a theoretical level in terms of the conflict—which is characteristic for architecture—between theoretical-academic knowledge and practical knowledge directed towards application. What is ultimately important is how these two forms of knowledge are synthesized.

How has your personal relationship to construction work changed? Do you still have time to follow what is happening on the sites of the many projects you are responsible for? Have your interests and decision criteria shifted with the development of your projects?
I think you have to be clearly oriented toward the actual practice of construction. Unfortunately I don't always have the opportunity to personally follow what is happening on specific projects. Yet although my interests and the questions I pose at the theoretical level have changed, the realization of theoretical insights at a practical level, or rather at the level of realization, remains a focus of my interest in architecture. I don't think my decision criteria have changed, but they have shifted to another level of understanding on the basis of the experience I've accumulated.

At what point are you certain that a particular architectural decision is the right one? How great is your need to question decisions on the construction site? Or put another way, as an architect, how does one maintain the greatest possible scope for action during the construction process?
There is no moment of certainty that an architectural decision is the right one. On the contrary, the finished building constantly teaches you that there could have been something better. I'm constantly confronted with this conflict. It's what makes developing and making a decision such a strenuous process. Nevertheless, I'm very conscious of my values regarding certain materials and proportionalities or concepts of space, and they inform my opinion of what is good or bad during the planning process. However, you always know you could do everything better. And that's why after one project you move on to another. If you no longer see yourself as being better in your next project, then you should probably stop being an architect. In this sense, the idea of finding something good is a constant struggle around that argument. So my need to question decisions during construction is a ubiquitous, constant, continual part of my work, and it takes a lot of self-discipline to keep myself from constantly airing these considerations or attempting to implement them. The question as to how an architect can maintain the greatest possible scope for action during the construction phase

is relatively simple to answer. It's too late! In reality, the fundamental aim is to have all questions resolved prior to beginning building, while at the same time you're certain that in the course of construction you'll gain insights that could push decisions in another direction.

What sort of preconditions does the Chinese building industry have to deal with? What sort of problems need to be solved there? What will your contribution to China be and what influences are you bringing back with you to Europe?
The main preconditions the Chinese building industry has to deal with are on the one hand the legal framework, which now is very similar to that found in Europe, and on the other the actual technical knowledge that skilled laborers and others involved in construction work are equipped with. This differs as much in China as it does in Europe. Differences between Switzerland and Holland are at least as great as those between Holland and China. Our contribution in China will undoubtedly involve the attempt to create a more sustainable architecture so that a more sustainable engagement with form will become central. A sustainable engagement with form means that buildings are considered in the longer term, that they have a longer lifespan, lower energy consumption and a considerably greater emphasis on comfort. And what am I bringing back from China in terms of influences? China has a very specific culture involving values and conventions that initially seem foreign to us in Europe. Such values are evident in the different form of social coexistence of individual groups, in the different form of family organization, and in the historically different cultural arrangement of geometric forms. These, I believe, are the most fundamental aspects. What has become clear to me in China is the interaction between cultural convention and formal architectural expression, which in turn has to do with the existential question of the relationship between architecture and the public sphere. In this context architecture plays an important role for the cultural identity of a city, a region, a locality, a country. It is, so to speak, a central task. This contribution made by architecture has become much clearer to me in China, due to the difference in cultural preconditions, than it was for me previously in Europe.

The construction and investment markets are becoming more international and this is being accompanied by an increase in cross-cultural influences. What sort of opportunities and dangers do you see in this context?
The danger is that the result will be a kind of homogenized internationalization which no longer comprehends or promotes the cultural specificity of

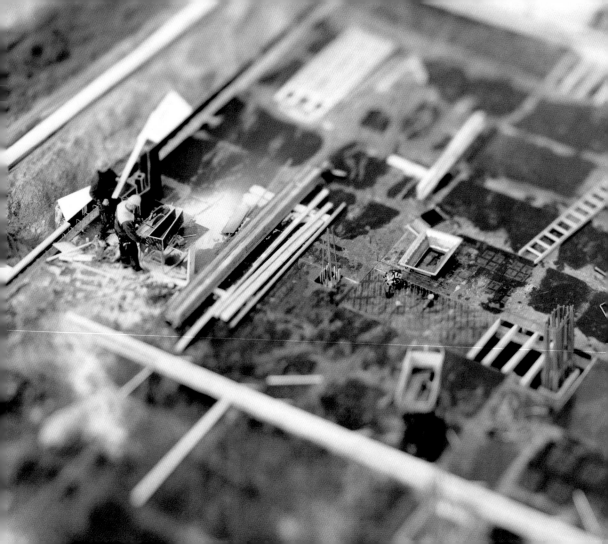

the locality, the region and the conventions associated with a particular place. What we in the 20th and 21st centuries are seeing is the second wave of internationalization. Behind us lies the fundamental postmodern critique of internationalization, which was mounted within the framework of modernity. Representatives of postmodernism explicitly pointed to specificity and the regional context. We find this, for example, in the work of Aldo Rossi and the architecture of Kenneth Frampton. In my opinion the danger now is that we will overlook specificity, with the result that this rather flat internationalization will be seen, wrongly, only as an opportunity and not as a risk. I am extremely critical of all architectural-theoretical approaches that take this supposedly international character as their point of departure, because they no longer see the fundamental reference system, namely the cultural conventions developed and specified by people over centuries as their point of departure and as the goal of architecture. In my view, the homogenization and interchangeability of images that is evident in the internet does not represent a gain for architecture but a very significant potential danger. So much for the dangers! The opportunities undoubtedly lie in the possibilities of supporting and further developing the different points of departure, which can lead to ever more specific solutions. This is where I see the greatest opportunity but also the greatest danger in the conflict between identity and convention, on the one hand, and homogenization and interchangeability on the other.

What in your opinion is the architect's most fundamental influence compared with all other participants in the construction process? Will we encounter architects in the role of the classic master builder on the building sites of the future and how will they ensure that they have the necessary competence?
The architect's job requires him or her to formulate the vision into which all others have to integrate their work. In this sense, the central task of the architect is to generate the future perspective that forms the basis of every project and to describe the framework into which the contributions of all other participants in the construction process can be integrated. I think that the role of the architect has not been fixed over the centuries, but has been changed a great deal depending on the particular social context. Consequently, I find it difficult to speak of the classic master builder because it's something I've never experienced or known. It seems to me that the understanding of the architect's role has gone through many changes. When we're speaking about the construction site context, however, the feedback created by the materialization of what was previously thought creates an extremely

important source of experience that inevitably generates a future perspective. The danger, as already mentioned, is that a reference to the building site is no longer necessary for the generation of generally valid and nonspecific images. I regard this as a fundamental loss in terms of architectural quality.

We are seeing a tendency for large building firms to diversify and look for business opportunities on both sides of the construction phase, i.e., in the fields of project development and facility management, because of the economic potential involved. Construction as such is at the mercy of a business cycle that is changing ever more quickly and it's now tied to a high degree of entrepreneurial risk for building firms. Where do you see dangers and opportunities for architects in the context of these developments? In principle that is the case, construction is increasingly being regarded as an economic asset and ever more subject to economic use and short-term planning. That is why we are seeing the tendency toward project development and facility management. The background to this development is the change in the role of the client. Whereas previously the traditional client was a concrete person or at least concretely personified, the processes of economic use are resulting in the client becoming anonymous. Now the clients are foundations or various investment funds, which are not represented by any single person. And yet it is only a person who is able to represent something. In my opinion this constitutes a negative development for our society, because it means that the connection between the building, the location and the people involved in the construction is increasingly being lost. I see more dangers than opportunities in this development. The long-term assessment of a building is now exclusively tied to its market value. However, changes in the market value are no longer attributed to the process of time but to the building itself, which in my view is wrong. Here I see a great danger. I believe that dealing with properties in this way means that in the longer term we will not be able to create cities that generate identity and thus have the potential to become homes and sources of solidarity.

You are someone who also sets great store by aesthetics. When does beauty emerge in architecture? If the question of beauty were that easy to answer, then we would all build much more beautiful houses than we have in fact done. I think the question of beauty needs to be answered on several levels. There is a personal level of experiencing beauty, which, as in the case of art, says more about the beholder than the object. And beyond this level, there is the question of how beauty emerges in the case of each project. Beauty is generated in the contribution a project makes, which goes beyond its immediate use value, namely in its contribution to the public sphere. This contribution to the public sphere—understood in terms of its relationship to the conventions or the history that determines that public sphere—presumably gives the building its societal significance as something that is regarded as beautiful or not beautiful. If the word "beauty" is taken as referring to something that moves people on a collective level and generates quality, then this does not only concern the current situation but also has a very pronounced temporal dimension. Such beauty is not something that is subject at certain points to particular fashions, but something that is in principle a contribution to the public sphere.

What for you is the most exciting moment within the cycle of a project, the promise of a project at its outset, its development, its emergence on the building site, or the moment when it is handed over and released into the everyday world? Or put another way, what is it that excites you the most about having constantly new projects?
The most exciting moments within the cycle of a project are undoubtedly the development of the project and the intellectual formulation of the utopia or, as we called it earlier, the vision which ultimately makes it possible for different people to work on such a project as an integrated whole. The material expression of this process is the construction site. The construction site repre-sents the emergence and examination of this previously formulated goal or vision. On the construction site all the essential moments that will ultimately generate quality are already discernible—in terms of suitability to the context of daily life, emotional reception and material longevity. In this sense what excites me the most is the process of emergence, in which the construction site becomes an image and an initial materialization of the process of intellectually developing the project.

In the sense of an examination?
No, in the sense of an initial materialization. "Examination" is perhaps the wrong word. What I'm referring to is a process of becoming visible, a verification of the idea or vision. What excites me most about constantly taking on new projects is the challenge of always having to learn how to deal with different forms of interaction, conventions, etc. The fact that new projects repeatedly confront me with different people and values is something I consider a great privilege.

Which of your projects do you see as exhibiting the greatest degree of correspondence between your ideas and expectations and the end results, which of them as exhibiting the least degree of correspondence, and what are the most important criteria in this respect?
I can't really answer that question because I'm disappointed in all my projects and understand them only as the promise of a better future.

Is there any particular historical age in which you would rather have worked?
My answer to that is an emphatic no! For me the age in which we are living —even though architecture is currently in a phase of reorientation and transition—is the situation I find best.

How would you describe your office's "project book"? Is it a compendium of rules developed on the basis of your experiences of building?
The project book in my office is not a compendium of rules for the practice of architecture but an attempt to formulate planning processes and methods that make it easier to achieve the goals I've already referred to. In this sense, the aim of the project book is not to chart a certain practice or method but rather to determine how practices can be made more goal-orientated. The project book is an attempt at communication between those who, so to speak, formulate the vision and those who help to implement this vision and make it reality. It attempts to engage more specifically with the interface problem in order to hone the process that begins with the idea and ends with its material realization.

What do you see as the outstanding achievements in the building technology field that are relevant to the demands you see as being placed on construction now and in the future? Are there production processes in other industries that the building industry can learn from? What do you see as constituting innovation in the construction field?
The outstanding achievement in the field of construction technology is the development of new materials that allow for different relationships to space. At the same time, I think the question of the extent to which such new achievements actually facilitate new architectural ways of seeing is one we will increasingly have to deal with in the future. The question as to the relationship between achievements in the field of construction technology and prevailing demands is really a chicken-and-egg question. It is probably a dialectical process in which both lines of development constantly move forward and change in parallel while also reinforcing one

another. The fact that this process is an extremely slow one and often proceeds in the wrong direction is shown by developments over the last 50 years. The quality of building around 1900 was probably better than what we have done over the last 50 years. In quantitative terms, what we did in the second half of the 20th century was extremely successful. But in qualitative terms, the current state of building raises more questions than it answers. In my view, this historical transitional situation is particularly evident in the development of building technology, because we are facing enormous technological changes—based on the development of new materials and the possibilities of formal expression being generated. The automobile industry has been a key factor in shaping modernity, but I don't believe current production processes in other leading industrial fields such as data processing allow for inferences relating to the building industry, even if we are repeatedly seeing the attempt to establish a kind of parallelism in the formal expression of projects. In my opinion the qualities of materials such as weight, hardness and mechanical resistance, i.e., their specific characteristics, which can be described relatively easily in colloquial terms, are ultimately more important for the wider development of the building industry. I don't believe in a "de-materialization" of architecture. On the contrary, I think that the yearning for de-materialization, which is expressed in the increasingly central role of digital imagery, will lead to a much more pronounced and more aware materialization of architecture. This seems interesting to me; such a development attests to the self-confidence I think our discipline needs to rely on its own strengths and find these in history.

Nowadays you build all over the world. Do you have a dream site you would like to build on?
I don't think I have a dream site; I find it exciting when the site presents real difficulties and complications. I'm interested in the intellectual challenge this presents me with and my ability to deal with this challenge accordingly.

CHAP. 04

THE CONSTRUCTION SITE PAST, PRESENT AND FUTURE

PROFESSIONAL PERSPECTIVES

In conversation: Margrit Bion (architect, Managing Director of Steiner GmbH, Deutschland), *Beat Büchler* (economist, Managing Director of the Swiss General Contractors Association VSGU and the Swiss Building Industry Group SBI), *Paul Meyer* (architect, Professor (emeritus) of Building Realisation at the ETH Zurich)
Moderation: Marie Antoinette Glaser

What does it mean for you to be on a building site? Do you feel a sense of fascination, or is it just part of your everyday work?

BEAT BÜCHLER (BB): The building site is a construction firm's most effective calling card. It immediately reveals the business culture of the firm involved.
Is there a sense of order, of logically organized action? Are the workers wearing helmets and proper work clothes? Are these labeled and is the machinery labeled? Over 30 years of experience in the construction sector have shown me that construction sites reveal the quality of a firm and its management.
The building site is the nuts and bolts—it shows how a firm works. We try to explain to the firms how important it is that a building site is tidy and

that work is obviously thoroughly organized. This is still not the case every-where. As a rule, building firms don't advertise. The construction site is their public face, and this is something that's not been recognized widely enough.

MARGRIT BION (MB): I see the building site from a different perspective. For me, what is important is whether the various aspects of the work process are correctly organized. My experience tells me what is working properly and where there are problems. I quickly get an impression of whether the construction site is under control or not, whether the planning is being implemented, or whether there isn't any planning at all. When construction sites are not functioning properly then the planning is faulty—or the plan is not being implemented. A sense of order is of course important, but when you yourself are involved but have come onto the site late in the process and face all sorts of coordination problems, then the situation looks a bit different.

PAUL MEYER (PM): I'm going to take the viewpoint of the building client here. For one major building client I've represented, there's always the danger that their representatives only monitor the building site from inside their offices. But when it comes to major projects, clients need to know how things are actually functioning on the site. In the case of one major project, we therefore stipulated in the general contractor agreement that the managing director of the building firm, the senior site manager and the canton master builder should accompany me on a tour of the building site lasting several hours every three months and discuss any problems over lunch that still hadn't been solved. As a result, when it came to the final review, there were no unresolved issues that had to be dealt with and no requests for additions. In the case of large building projects, it's important that not only the architect but also the foremen of all participating engineering firms be present on the site. Updated schedules, blueprints and plans for skills coordination need to be hanging in plain view in site offices. Regarding your statement about the importance of whether a building site is tidy or not, I think the potential for accidents is also a key point. A lack of safety fences or iron lying around represents real problems. When it comes to order on a site, it's not just a matter of the visual aspect but also safety. An ordered site is not only a marketing tool but also a safety precaution. It means that client representatives and in particular site managers aren't threatened with jail due to accidents.

That's why our firm's major building sites are subject to a strict risk review every month. In addition, an independent security officer monitors the building sites.

BB: The premiums charged by the Swiss Accident Insurance Fund (SUVA) rise sharply in cases of damage. So firms have a solid financial reason to minimize accidents.

PM: Building construction is much more complex than underground construction is in that sense. A large building site can have up to 500 people working on it at the same time. If the site management doesn't have complete control over the various aspects of the project, the result is chaos. Apart from accidents, quarrels can break out, even fights between crane operators, who'll go at each other with their cranes.

What about the diversity of building site culture? Are time and performance pressures having a strong influence on the way work is done and organized?

PM: The culture of the construction site has fundamentally changed over the last 30 years. Fewer and fewer components are actually being manufactured on site, practically none, with the exception of on-site concrete, and even that is now supplied in semi-finished form. This means planning has to be more precise. Today, the assembly of prefabricated components is increasingly being done by unskilled laborers. Previously nearly all dryliners were carpenters. These days laborers from other countries are given short-term training, work for piece rates and have no interested in coordinating with contractors working on the same project. They have no idea where the work of the different trades overlaps. Previously, consultation and collaboration between the different trades represented on a site were taken for granted. The current situation has to do with pricing pressures. The cheapest workers are employed to deliver the prefabricated components and assemble them.

BB: It is true that the number of people employed in the major building trades is constantly shrinking, even in a boom period. The reason is that many are only given short-term contracts. It used to be the case that workers would come from Italy, Spain and Portugal and had a certain professional pride. They took pleasure in doing good work. This is hardly ever the case today.

PM: They are under a lot of pressure, too.

MB: In Germany the pressure and price wars are much more severe than here in Switzerland. We worked on a building for Swiss Life in Munich. The construction firm brought workers from Poland and the Czech Republic to do the underground work and the entire basement construction. A group like this consists of between 100 and 150 workers. The live in barracks and have a cook and a translator. It's like a package. They stay for three months, do the structural work, are fed and housed, and then leave. Then another group arrives. The difficult thing is that we can't communicate directly with them. We need a translator. And although they have some training, they haven't got our trade skills.

PM: The construction firms are working more cheaply and efficiently. Fewer people means higher turnover. This has an effect on the quality. Three times as much is being produced today than 30 years ago. This is connected with the development of prefabricated components but also with the enormous deadline pressure on building sites. However, the tendency to build more quickly is not only based on cost. In recent years building has not become a great deal more expensive; it's the land that has really gone up in price. A large part of the money that clients pay out today is for building plots. Once the property has been acquired, most clients want to see building start the next day, because interest is already beginning to accumulate. And when interest on building loans and mortgages rises, this means even greater deadline pressures for private building clients. And they often make the mistake of not planning well enough and this can lead to conflict on the site between building firms, architects and clients.

BB: I can confirm this from my own experience. Building firms often complain that they are put under enormous pressure although planning is non-existent or insufficient. It is very difficult to plan after the construction process has begun.

MB: It's a fatal mistake. It's been a problem in Germany for a long time now. Shortening the planning phase is a completely wrong approach. Constructing facades today is no longer possible without having overall concepts for the building and its energy use. Many building planners find this a strain because they haven't taken an interest in these aspects previously. Building sites can only function well if these questions are properly solved in the planning phase. If they aren't, serious problems arise.

PM: It's worth convincing clients that twice the amount of time needs to be invested in planning because they will save this time later during construction and get a better quality at a lower cost. This was my experience with the first and second stages of the Irchel University campus. The overall time for planning and construction was identical. But the longer planning time could be compensated for by a much shorter construction time in the second stage.

Why has time pressure on projects increased?

MB: In the private sector, projects move through the different stages of the construction process much more quickly, while at the same time demands have become more complex. Communicating with the increased number of participants in the construction process takes up a lot of time.

PM: The short amount of time available for actual construction also has to do with long building-approval procedures and decision processes that have become much more complex. I do not envy the construction firms. There doesn't seem to be much room for unhurried, enjoyable work.

BB: I often hear the complaint that it takes an enormously long time to get the actual go-ahead. And once the decision is made, work is supposed to start at eight the next morning. And then nothing happens because preparations for construction haven't proceeded far enough.

MB: But why is the building industry subject to such low prices? Why does it sell itself so badly? A Swiss lawyer can demand 200 to 500 francs an hour.

BB: There are no barriers to entry. If a business with a hundred employees goes bankrupt today, then tomorrow there will be ten businesses with ten employees. That's the reason for the low level of pricing. Even today, when we are seeing a boom in building construction, prices have not improved.

PM: The level of solidarity within the building industry is low. Bids are too low, even in the case of individual fees. People are constantly underbidding one another. This doesn't have to be the case. If everyone on the market raised their prices by ten percent, clients would have to pay.

BB: It's a question of differentiation and specialization. In the planning area it's easier to differentiate yourself. However, in the construction area, everyone can do brickwork. I was recently at a conference where people were complaining again about prices. Someone suggested that building firms should start developing projects themselves. This would mean of course that general contractors would come under pressure in the area they call their own. It's a difficult situation.

PM: At one point there was a lot of discussion of the „Build Smart!" approach. The idea was to bring together skilled-trades groups. Such an arrangement could result in better integrated construction sites and improve quality while also providing a cost-effective solution from the warranty perspective. I believe that building clients would give work to such groups.

BB: But it can't function because each firm wants to realize a profit. You need a general contractor who assumes overall responsibility.

MB: The building world in Berlin is fairly rough and ready. In some cases we have awarded contracts for modules. In the case of a hotel in Potsdam we ended up with four sub-sub-sub-subcontractors. It doesn't necessarily work.

Is amalgamation a strategy that small and medium-sized building enterprises should adopt?

BB: It is quite possible for a smaller building firm with the right staff to take on the tasks of a general contractor. It doesn't always have to be a huge project; it might be a one-family house.

MB: I don't completely share your opinion. A mid-sized building firm, of which there are not many left, is better off establishing a partnership with a general contractor. The general contractor does not of course do the work itself. To be a „total service contractor" today, one which undertakes planning and building and assumes all the responsibility, the contractor needs a building firm or a master builder as a partner with the necessary know-how and qualified people.

BB: Building firms usually have mixed feelings about entering partnerships with general contractors. General contractors are professional experts that award contracts. They know the pricing situation.

MB: But perhaps they have more interesting projects. A master builder can't do everything.

PM: Take a look at underground construction. There you find lots of joint ventures. Why shouldn't that be possible in the building construction field?

BB: The joint-venture model is actually a faulty one, because it gives rise to additional interfaces and costs. It really developed out of the desire of public clients to satisfy a range of parties. But it would be more efficient and effective if one party alone took on the whole project.

MB: A building involves different types of work. If these can be well combined, all parties can benefit.

How would you summarize the developments that the building industry will face in the coming years?

PM: In other countries we are seeing a strong tendency towards larger firms. In the medium term in Switzerland, both large general contractors and small and mid-sized firms will continue to exist side by side.

BB: One economic theory argues that there's a general tendency for very large firms to develop and for the mid-sized sector to decline. Small firms, on the other hand, can survive because they have their established niches.

BB: In Switzerland we are also seeing now a tendency toward public-private partnerships, with responsibility for financing often assumed by a consortium. England is a prime example in this regard. In Switzerland an initial project has been launched, a school in Langenthal. It is hoped that this successful example will result in the PPP model being more widely used. However, it requires projects of a particular size.

PM: I'm skeptical. I would rather stick with the old model. If clients also delegate financing then in a certain sense they are disempowering themselves.

PPP also means circumventing GATT rules. If at least 51 percent of financing comes from private sources then the rules no longer apply. In this regard, Switzerland has unfortunately caused problems for itself by accepting these rules and upholding them. I have never heard of an appeal being lodged in another European country on the basis of noncompliance with these rules.

What sorts of difficulties are faced by Swiss firms trying to establish themselves in other markets?
BB: Anyone who wants to be successful has to acquire a local firm or a share of one. Being active in the major building trades while using Switzerland as a base is not without its problems because companies need a maintenance depot for machinery. Working across borders, on the other hand, doesn't work.
PM: At most when the areas are closely situated. For example, southern German firms work in Switzerland. And firms from the Fricktal region work in the Black Forest. The people speak almost the same dialect. But when greater distances are involved it doesn't work. Following the oil shock in the 1970s, many construction firms had problems with contracts. Major firms in Switzerland such as Elektrowatt worked as far afield as the Middle East. All of them returned burdened with debt. For this reason I think that in the building trades local knowledge plays an important role, whether in regard to local regulations or relations between everyone working on the construction site.

How are new technologies and electronic means of communication influencing construction sites, and what sort of effect will they have in the future?
MB: Everything will become quicker but also more secure. The Olmero construction tendering platform and other such tools, which enable all participants to access data and plans, are simplifying many aspects. On the other hand, the pace of everything could speed up. Everyone can now be reached by mobile phone and decisions will be expected in a matter of minutes.
PM: New technologies will make planning work and coordination much simpler. On the other hand, I'm not sure whether automation in the building industry has a future on the building site. Concrete constructions are difficult to prefabricate. Two young assistant professors in the architecture faculty at ETH have built a robot that can lay bricks. But it remains to be seen whether it is worth using such expensive computer-controlled robots for relatively simple manual work. I think it is rather the case that planning needs to be perfected.
BB: There is still a lot of potential in the field of knowledge management. If a database is available that provides access to information on a particular

product, its applications and associated problems, then that would seem to me to be an important step towards improving efficiency. Furthermore, it should be possible, for example, for parts of a structure to be copied for use in other projects on the basis that they have already functioned well in one context and can be made available like a module. The tragedy is that we always assume there must be a unique solution. But why?

MB: Because every house looks different!

PM: Every building plot is different. There are forward-looking enterprises such as the Baumschlager & Eberle architectural firm, which has built up a computerized library of details. The different constructions are integrated into each new design, such that it is precisely tailored to the particular situation. This means they can work more quickly and cost-effectively.

I've heard that in Tokyo there are building sites worked on by robots and machines. What do you think of this?

PM: As long as the building shell is still constructed using job-mixed concrete, I don't think that robots will be able to do this work. As long as job-mixed concrete is cheaper than steelwork and solves more problems, prefabrication remains difficult. On the other hand, one could envisage using robots for steelwork. But steelwork is expensive because it needs a lot of energy and above all insulation against noise. It seems to me that there is more potential for the use of robots in timber-frame construction.

Will more women work on building sites in the future?

MB: There are still relatively few of us with positions in the building industry, and I hope that more women will enter our profession. Women in the building industry need to have their feet firmly on the ground. The need to be able to fight for what they want and show they have the necessary know-how. Of course, this also applies to men, but when a woman wants to enter the male domain of building, she usually finds five men in front of her. A woman needs to fight to get a start in this industry.

BB: It is pleasing to see that more women are becoming involved in the building industry. I know of a range of cases where women are driving trucks or operating cranes. Mechanization and the introduction of new devices and machines means that women's physical disadvantage isn't as significant anymore. There is a positive trend in the interior construction trade, where women are becoming more and more numerous.

MB: I can only encourage women to make their way in the industry.

CHAP. 05

SWEATY WORK

A BUILDING SITE PEON REPORTS

Mikael Krogerus

I am on a building crane, 40 m above the ground. My hands are clinging to the rungs of the ladder, I'm sweating, my legs feel weak and my heart is racing. The steel supports seem to be tilting, my vision flickers. Don't let go, I say aloud. The crane cabin seems to be miles above me. It all began when a cultural studies scholar from ETH asked me if as a journalist I would be interested in working on a building site for several days and then writing a report about it. At the time it sounded like an opportunity to drink beer, develop a few manly calluses and earn some easy money. Six months later I find myself at Kloten Airport. The object of my investigation is located between the parking deck and the arrival level, the building site of the Radisson SAS Airport-Hotel Zurich on land owned by Unique (Zurich – Flughafen AG). It is my task to investigate the everyday world of the building site for a book by the ETH academic. It is a chance to find the answers to some of the really big questions. What really goes on behind construction hoarding? What does a foreman actually do? Where does a crane operator take a pee? What sort of processes does building work involve? What sort of hierarchies develop? Are there women on a building site? A sign announces who is building here (Karl Steiner AG), what is being built (airport hotel) and until when (summer 08). Three cranes tower over the site, standing motionless against the cold morning sky like secularized minarets of modernity. I spot a crane operator slowly beginning the ascent to his cabin. I feel dizzy.

Behind the fence, site trailers obscure the view of the building pit. Eugenio Quadraccia, the 33-year-old site manager from Calabria, greets me and looks me over. He briefly criticizes my footwear, then gives me a helmet and rain gear and leads me to the crime scene. It is my first construction site and what a site it is: a hundred meters long and a hundred meters wide. The construction pit must be 20 m deep. Formwork carpenters, concreters, steel

fixers, masons and foremen move everywhere like ants. Three levels are being worked on at once: the construction pit, the ground floor, and the first upper floor. Further stories are to follow. The 75 x 75 m cube has been under construction since May 2006. It is destined to be a hotel made of a great deal of concrete, steel and glass, with 329 rooms, a conference center, three office levels, two restaurants and a lounge, as well as entertainment facilities in the basement. ACRON L & R, a real estate holding from Düsseldorf, is investing 154 million Swiss francs in the building.

I am immediately struck by just how many people work here and how quick they are. The construction workers I am familiar with are the ones that drop metal pipes clanging to the ground outside my window at seven in the morning or tear up the streets, bare-chested in the hot sun, and block the traffic. But here, hidden behind the hoarding, everything is different. Unseen by the public, real craftsmanship is being practiced. The workers move like ballet dancers in a choreographed rhythm. They push, form, hoist, dig, fix steel

and mix concrete. You can't exactly imagine them singing and performing pirou-
ettes with the wheelbarrows, but there is something almost elated about the
way they work.

Quadraccia leads me across the site: "This is the construction pit. There
you see concreting, over there is bricklaying, and here they're putting up
formwork." The pace of work is fast. The building shell needs to be completed
by October 2007. On a single day ten to 15 tons of steel and around
80 m3 of concrete are set in place. Quadraccia reckons they will need 25,000 m^3
of concrete for the whole hotel. Compare this to the 600 m^3 need for a
one-family house! Above our heads the cranes swing around, elegantly moving
loads weighing several tons and depositing them with unbelievable preci-
sion between workers and metal rods. Fifty workers are on the site; 24 belong
to the building contractor Anliker, the rest to subcontractors, such as
the one responsible for steel fixing. Helmet colors indicate the hierarchy of positions: the subcontractors wear yellow and blue, the foremen and leading
hands red, and the site and project managers white. The subcontractors work
on a piece-rate basis and are paid for every square meter or kilogram
built. The predominant dialect on the site is Thuringian. Most of the limited-
contract workers come from eastern Germany.
　　The brains behind this detailed choreography is Remo Monn, one of the two
site foremen. He is a likeable guy with spiky hair and a preference for
hip-hop trousers. Remo—people use first names on the site—is 21 and he is responsible for a logistical miracle. All the steel and concrete he orders must be
built into the structure that same day; the hotel is being fitted exactly into the
gap between the parking deck and the terminal. There is no space to store
material! It is also his task to ensure that work is organized in accordance with
the site manager's plans and to coordinate the leading hands. He orders
construction materials such as concrete, reinforcement and scaffolding, he
checks that everything is delivered and in the right amounts, and when he can
he joins in the work. He also has to deal with safety issues. Are there side
frames on all the scaffolds? Is the formwork stabile? Are the workers wearing
helmets and protective shoes? At the same time, he has to make sure that
costs are kept down and deadlines are kept in mind. Every day that construction
goes over the deadline is subject to a contractual penalty of 10,000 francs.
Remo tells me that his employer has never been late completing a construction
contract. This means that leading hands also face a lot of pressure to
keep up their teams' work rate. The normal working day is 8 hours, but here
everyone works 9 and often on Saturdays as well. Remo tells me, "At the
moment we are a bit behind schedule." The sand layer in the construction pit

was washed out by rain, resulting in a base failure that set work back by six weeks. The ground floor is more or less on schedule, and the first story is even a few days ahead.

Remo sits in a site trailer and broods over the construction drawings. The door continually opens. Just now a bricklayer has looked in to say that the ceiling of the ground floor seems to extend two centimeters too far out. Someone has probably calculated the wrong measurements, says Remo, but that's something for the geometricians to decide. He'll make an appointment with them for tomorrow. The small trailer is full of illegible notes and mysterious floor plan drawings. I'm just asking myself what I'm doing with a safety helmet when Bruno, one of the leading hands comes round the corner and says: "You wanna work?"

I'm sent up to the roof in order to "dig out" an incorrectly set steel girder. My weapon is a fierce-looking device, a type of mobile jackhammer made by the firm of Hilti; it weighs a good 10 kg and has an adjustable handle. As soon as it meets resistance it fires up. It drones and throbs and I can feel the heavy rebound down to my bones. It's a painful process. The Hilti keeps slipping to the side or hitting my foot. The concrete does not give way. A worker asks, "Whaddya taking so long for?" He takes the Hilti and drills large pieces out of the concrete—at a tempo that I could never reach in a lifetime of practice. Nevertheless, I try to imitate him and press down on the drill with all my strength. Fragments fly around me.

A gang of Portuguese workers are fixing steel nearby and they make fun of me in a friendly sort of way. Steel fixing is said to be among the hardest jobs on a building site. The men stand bent forward over the long steel struts and use a so-called iron bender to connect the individual steel rods to form a lattice. Even watching them makes my back ache. How must they be feeling? I'm fascinated by their compact physiques: the large dirty hands, the broad, rounded shoulders and the powerful muscles outlined in their tight work clothes. Their eyes are narrowed to small slits to avoid the smoke from cigarettes hanging from the corners of their mouths. In Switzerland an unskilled laborer earns 23 to 25 francs an hour, a leading hand around 5,000 francs a months, a foreman between 6,500 and 8,500 francs.

Midday. I realize with relief that it is lunchtime and stagger behind my colleagues into the site trailer. Everyone unpacks their lunchboxes, eats large amounts of rye bread and cold meat and reads the free newspaper. Eddie says it's a „damn good paper." A lot of the men nod in agreement. Some talk about the job, but soon an exhausted silence spreads through the trailer. I don't ask what they wanted to be when they were kids or what they dream of doing now—my own fatigue stifles every journalistic impulse I might have. After what seems like an eternity, a bricklayer murmurs that he is going home on Friday and do we still want to do any concreting today? No one answers him. Bruno, the leading hand, makes notes on a punch list: observe safety precautions, maintain radio discipline. The leading hands have radios to guide the crane operators, Bruno explains. Instead of constantly radioing they should use the internationally recognized hand signals: rotating arm movements with the index finger pointing down = slowly downwards; rotating arm movements with the index finger pointing up = slowly upwards.

"Are there only men here?" I ask Remo on the way back to the construction site.

"Uh-huh."

"Why?"

"You need a certain amount of physical and mental robustness."

"Mental?"

"Most times the guys tell you what they think straight up, no chaser. That's not something for women."

I wonder to myself whether building sites mightn't function as protected zones for a masculinity threatened with extinction.

It is my second day on the site and I see a woman for the first time. The surveyor has arrived to measure the roof—a woman! Her beige jeans are stuffed into rubber boots and she looks like an aristocrat in jodhpurs—what a good idea of Remo's to call the surveyor! We all pause for a moment and look at her devoutly, marveling at the concentration with which she measures the area without dignifying us with even a glance. It is a matter of two centimeters. There is a murmur of innuendo, someone whistles. It has stopped raining and a few rays of sunlight break through the clouds. After two rainy days on the building site in an unfamiliar, rough male world, the woman seems to me like a ray of hope. I want to go over to her and ask her name, whether she will go out with me, whether she will be my wife.

Eddie awakens me from my reverie: "Hey, news guy, here's something for you to do." He gives me the task of precisely nailing small wooden boxes into the formwork. Concreting will begin tomorrow and the wooden boxes are needed to create gaps for the cable that will be laid later. Eddie demonstrates: fix three nails diagonally on three sides, hammer them in, and that's it. "Got it?"

"No problem," I say.

It certainly looks simple enough. But while I knew I wouldn't be able to do it as smoothly as Eddie, I didn't realize it would be impossible. Either I knock the nail right through the wood but not into the floor or the nail bends or the box slips. After I've banged around 33 nails into four boxes, Eddie comes by and complains about my lack of accuracy. I have to show him how I'm doing it. Nervously I line up a nail, swing back and hit it in crookedly with three blows. When I try to pull it out again, I manage to pull the whole box apart. Suddenly Bruno turns up and watches as I hit my thumb. Bruno keeps a straight face and says I should put my thumb above my head for a few minutes. I'll feel nauseous and a bit dizzy but that will pass. I follow his advice. The thumb swells and within a matter of minutes turns red, then blue, then red again. I take my hand down and the pain is actually gone. Once I'm alone again, things start to go better. Now I'm able to hit a nail (not the long ones) into the wood (but not from the side). I even get a vague idea of how exhilarating it must be to drive the nail in with a single stroke.

My time on the building site is nearing its end. Remo the foreman asks, "Have you been up the crane?"
"Nah, I was just planning to do that," I answer.
Bruno radios Max, the crane operator, "The news guy's coming up."

And so, in unpleasantly wet weather, I climb a crane. I act like James Bond but feel like Woody Allen. Eventually I reach the operator's cab. Max, a funny guy with long hair, is leaning nonchalantly on the railing around the tiny platform. I nearly embrace him with relief and tension rushes out of me in an uncoordinated flood of words. When I've calmed down a little, Max tells me he's been a crane operator for 13 years and that he likes listening to heavy metal. He never climbs down for lunch and pees in a plastic drink bottle. Then he lets me sit in the operator's seat. It's comfortable. A transistor radio is playing softly and the floor is transparent. There are two joysticks. The left-hand one is used to move the crane and the right-hand one to control the crane trolley. A monitor shows wind speed, load weight and height. I rotate the crane once on its axis, looking over Kloten Airport and then down onto "my" building site. It is wonderful to be able to recognize the ordered arrangement of work down to the last detail. I see the steel fixers weaving their lattice, which gradually becomes denser, while joiners pull boarding out of concreted walls—everyone is doing what they should be. I look down at the workers and move the mighty crane forwards and backwards. From this height any problems seem small, insignificant. I don't feel any vertigo anymore, I hardly feel any pain and I don't have any misgivings about my lack of manual skill. I look over the scene below me affectionately and for a wonderful moment I am happy. Max tells me he has to get back to work.

Recently I was on my building site again. It is not a building site anymore but half a building. Nearly three stories of the hotel now rise out of the

construction pit. The workers still remembered the „news guy" and greeted me warmly. Remo told me they would be ready by the middle of October. I felt mighty proud.

CHAP. 06

WORK IN PROGRESS

BUILDING SITE PORTRAITS

A new building begins with an excavation or a demolition—a process of dealing with either earth and rock or the fabric of an old building. Despite all the advantages that technology has brought, building remains complicated and unpredictable. Sophisticated plans need to be produced and implemented meticulously, costs estimated, risks calculated, people, machines and material organized, all under enormous time pressure. The sheer numbers that confront workers during a construction project are enormous. In a short time they construct buildings over an area equal to three, 13, or even a 113 football fields. They often have to work far into the night. Projects can involve dozens of cranes and diggers weighing up to 45 tons. The truckloads of debris that have to be carted away can number in the tens of thousands and even more those to transport to the site all the concrete, steel and glass needed. Often the building is being used by the old or new occupants while construction is going on.

Here, nine current, spectacular, major building sites in Switzerland and Europe are presented. They all have their own distinctive characteristics, whether these involve a central location in a thriving city, an especially complex undertaking, or remarkable proportions. They are all unique in terms of their materials and dimensions.

BMW WELT, MUNICH (D)

NEUE MESSE, STUTTGART (D)

EGLISE ST. SULPICE, PARIS (F)

LETZIGRUND-STADION, ZURICH (CH)

BELLEVUE-HAUS, ZURICH (CH)

WOHNPARK FELDHOF, ZUG (CH)

SPITAL LINTH, UZNACH (CH)

NEW RESIDENTIAL COMPLEX EICH-
WIESEN, FÄLLANDEN (CH)

SIHLCITY, ZURICH (CH)

Taiyo Onorato & Nico Krebs
Windows, 2005
C-Print, 75 x 90 cm

Gabriela Gerber und Lukas Bardill
Komatsu (detail)
In the administration building of Calanda Kieswerk AG Chur
Object, 245 parts (wall/ceiling version), 686 x 401 x 0,3 cm,
polychrome powder-coated sheet steel glued to concrete

NEW BUILDING INFORMATION AND DELIVERY CENTER FOR BMW

Greatest challenge
Complexity of the multifunctional building with 1147 rooms

Client: BMW AG
Architects: Coop Himmelb(l)au
Construction workers: 600
Hours of work: Monday to Saturday, 6 am – 10 pm
Area: 25 000 m² ≈ 3½ football fields
Excavation pit: 15 579 m² ≈ 2 football fields
Excavation volume: 155 000 m³ ≈ 13 000 truckloads
Reinforcing steel: 9000 t
Rod steel: 3 000 000 m, manually laid
Steel construction: above zero 4500 t ≈ ½ Eiffel Tower
Concrete: 60 000 m³ ≈ a block measuring 39 x 39 x 39 m
Glass: 14 500 m²
Tower Cranes: 8 in peak periods, Liebherr
Construction time: 4 years (2003 – 2007)
Total investment: over 150 000 000 CHF

NEUE MESSE, STUTTGART (D):

A NEW TRADE-FAIR CENTER: GERMANY'S LARGEST BUILDING SITE

Greatest challenge
Constructing a six-story parking lot using the incremental launching method over Germany's busiest highway while it is in use.

Client: Projektgesellschaft Neue Messe GmbH & Co. KG
Construction firms: 1000
Architects: wulf & ass. Architekten GmbH
Construction workers: up to 1700, over 10 000 in total
Hours of work: multi-shift
Area: 830 000 m² ≈ 113 football fields
Languages spoken: 15
Excavation volume: 1 800 000 m³ ≈ 180 000 truck journeys ≈ a line of trucks from Stuttgart to Madrid; approx. 190 truckloads per day
Steel: 65 000 t ≈ 8½ Eiffel Towers
Concrete: 600 000 m³ ≈ a block measuring 84 x 84 x 84 m
Glass facades: 40 000 m²
Electric cable: 3 600 000 m ≈ Strecke the distance from Norway to Africa
Tower cranes: 70 in peak periods, Liebherr (and others)
Construction machines: 200 in peak periods
Construction time: 3 years (2004 – 2007)
Total investment: 1 209 000 000 CHF

EGLISE ST. SULPICE, PARIS (F):

ONE OF THE MOST COMPREHENSIVE RESTORATIONS OF A LISTED BUILDING IN FRANCE

Greatest challenge
Replacing the patchwork concrete with stone without damaging the underlying material

Client: Lefèvre
Architect: Hervé Baptiste
Area: 182,25 m²
Tower hight: 71 m
Masonry: Replacing 6 t wall sections and 3 m high evangelist figures each weighing 60 t
Tower cranes: Liebherr
Construction time: estimated 4 years (2006 – 2010)
Total investment: 42 000 000 CHF

NEW BUILDING MULTIFUNCTIONAL STADIUM

Greatest challenge
Commencing construction while stadium in use, difficult steel construction

Management contractor: Implenia Generalunternehmung AG
Client: City of Zurich
Architects: Bétrix & Consolascio Architekten AG, Frei & Ehrensperger
Construction workers: 250 to 350
Area: 64 000 m² ≈ 9 football fields
Excavation volume: 280 000 m³, 150 to 200 truckloads per day. A quarter of the excavated material will be processed on site for the new building, which will save 15 000 additional truckloads
Steel girders: 31, each 45 m long, up to 52 t
Wood: 23 000 m³ for the inner cladding of the stadium roof = 50 x 50 mm slats of Hungarian acacia wood, to be attached by 80 timber construction specialists with 320 000 screws
Construction time: 21 months (2005 – 2007)
Total investment: 121 000 000 CHF

BELLEVUE-HAUS, ZURICH (CH):

REVITALIZATION: COMPLETE RENOVATION, INCLUDING PARTIAL RECONSTRUCTION AND CONSTRUCTION OF A NEW SUBLEVEL

Greatest challenge

Dealing with poor substratum and static building fabric, implementing historical listing specifications and requirements of fire safety authorities, safety requirements in a building that includes tenant occupancy and an exposed area around the structure

General contractor: Implenia Generalunternehmung AG
Client: AG Bellevue c/o UBS AG
Chief architect: Martin Spühler Architekt BSA SIA
Participating firms: 35
Construction workers: approx. 60
Hours of work: Monday to Friday, 6 am – 5:30 pm
Foundation piles: approx. 230 piles to support additional loads in poor substratum, each 20 m long
Bracing: approx. 200 tonnes of steel fitted temporarily to support the aboveground levels
Construction time: estimated 3 years (2006 – 2009)
Total investment: 50 000 000 CHF

WOHNPARK FELDHOF, ZUG (CH):

CONSTRUCTION OF A RESIDENTIAL COMMUNITY WITH 14 BUILDINGS AND 364 APARTMENTS
(265 CONDOMINIUMS AND 99 RENTAL APARTMENTS)

Greatest challenge
Satisfying the wishes of 265 apartment buyers, who are the actual clients

Client: Alfred Müller AG
Architects: KBCG Architekten – Zwimpfer Partner (competition project),
Müller + Partner Architekten AG (development and implementation)
Area: 40 000 m² ≈ 6 football fields
Reinforcing steel: 4200 t ≈ ½ Eiffel Tower
Concrete: 48 000 m³ ≈ a block measuring 36 x 36 x 36 m
Construction time: estimated 6 years (2002 – 2008)
Total investment: 240 000 000 CHF

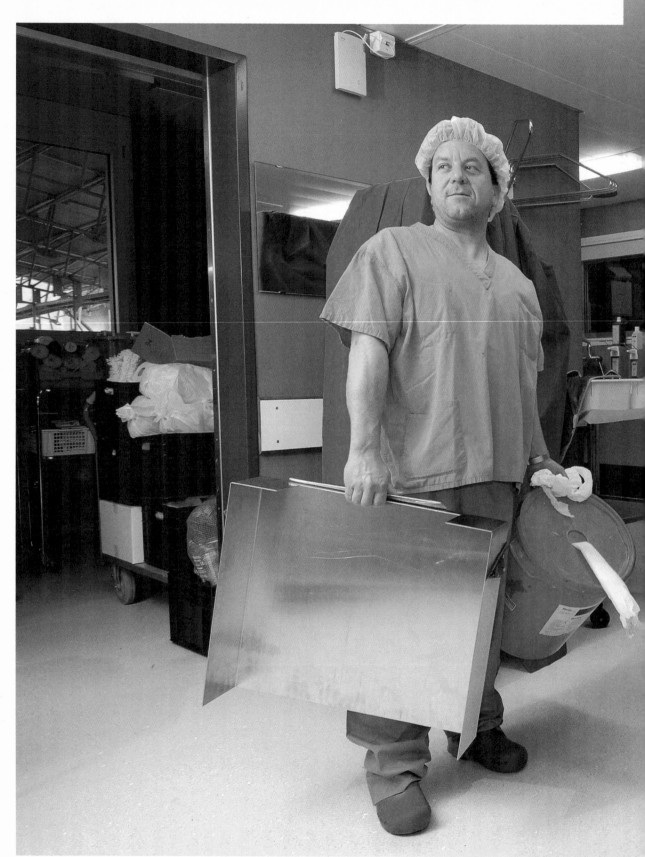

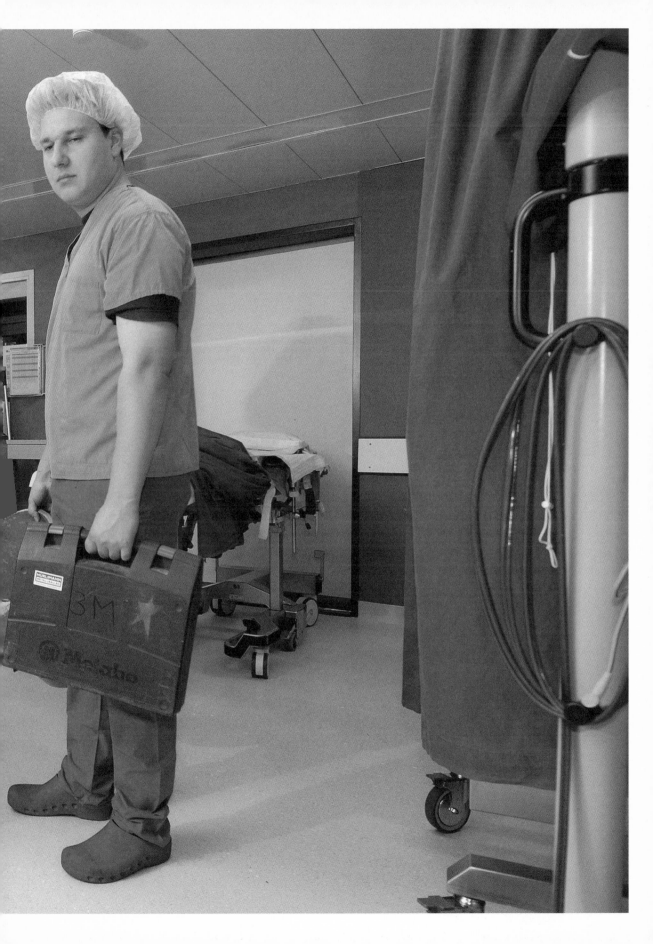

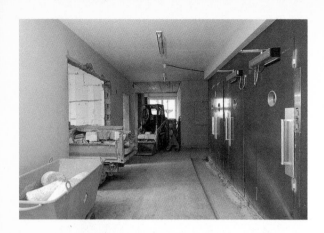

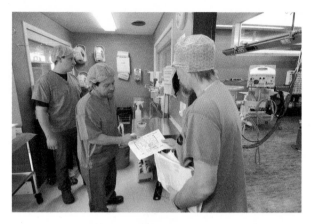

HOSPITAL RECONSTRUCTION

Greatest Challenge
Reconstructing the individual levels while hospital in use, supplying levels via a building facade lift

Building firm: Feldmann Bau AG Bilten
Client: Hochbauamt St. Gallen, Spitalbauten
Participating firms: 90 to 100
Architects: Itten + Brechbühl AG
Construction workers: 30 to 50
Hours of work: Monday to Friday, 8 am – 11:30 am, 2 pm – 5:45 pm
(time limits on noisy work, hourly breaks, afternoon rest break must
be observed)
Steel: 111,6 t
Concrete: approx. 700 m³ ≈ a block measuring 9 x 9 x 9 m
Cranes: 1, hook clearance 48 m
Buidling facade lift: load capacity 2400 kg, speed 70 cm per sec.
Construction time: estimated 6 years (2006 – 2012)
Total investment: Stage 1 (2006 – 2008): 35 000 000 CHF

NEW RESIDENTIAL COMPLEX EICHWIESEN, FÄLLANDEN (CH):

erschiedene Arten zu sein.

NEW RESIDENTIAL COMPLEX

Greatest challenge
Logistics and construction sequence

Building firm: Feldmann Bau AG Bilten
Concrete gravel supplier: KIBAG
Construction workers: approx. 250
Architects: Tilla Theus und Partner AG, Burkhalter und Partner AG,
Frei Architekten AG, Dettli Nussbaumer Architekten GmbH
Area: approx. 95 000 m² ≈ 13 football fields
Excavation volume: 120 000 m³, 100 truckloads per day
Steel: 3700 t ≈ ½ the Eiffel Tower
Concrete: 36 000 m³ ≈ a block measuring 33 x 33 x 33 m
Mixed gravel/concrete gravel: 48 000 m³ ≈ a block measuring 36 x 36 x 36 m
Cranes: 12 top-slewing cranes
Construction machines: approx. 15; diggers: 2,5 to 45 t
Prefabricated concrete supports: 600
Facade scaffold: 59 000 m²
Construction time: estimated 2 years (2006 – 2008)
Total investment: 180 000 000 CHF

Betreten der
Baustelle verboten

Bei Unfällen wird jede
Haftung abgelehnt

SHOPPING/RESIDENTIAL/CULTURE/LEISURE/HEALTH: SWITZERLAND'S LARGEST PRIVATE CONSTRUCTION PROJECT

Greatest challange:
Communications and logistics

Developer and management contractor: Karl Steiner AG
Client: Miteigentümergemeinschaft Sihlcity, Zurich, represented by
Credit Suisse and Swiss Prime Site AG
Architects: Theo Hotz AG
Construction workers: 300 to 600
Area: 41991 m² ≈ 6 football fields
Aushubvolumen: 140000 m³ ≈ 10000 truck journeys, a third of which to
dispatch station only; 2500 journeys with contaminated material originating
from the paper factory originally on the site
Concrete: over 100000 m³, 1800 m³ per day ≈ a block measuring 12 x 12 x 12 m
Cranes: up to 13
Construction time: nearly 4 years (2003 – 2007)
Total investment: 600000000 CHF, excl. tenant

CHAP. 07

Dieter Leistner
Blaue Serie, 1994
c print, 100 x 120 cm

Dieter Leistner
Blaue Serie, 1994
c print, 100 x 120 cm

A CONSTRUC-TION SITE BEGINS LONG BEFORE THE NOISE

COMMUNICATING CONSTRUC-TION PROJECTS

Markus Zimmermann und Hans Conrad Daeniker
With excerpts from a discussion with Peter Zeugin (a sociologist who works in the field of real estate development strategies in the private building sector)

From the charm of the arcane to market event

Hans Conrad Daeniker: "Construction sites are mysterious, forbidden. You see half-naked building workers who speak foreign languages and drink straight from the bottle. They climb down into filthy ditches where cables snake about and disappear into holes... That is my childhood memory of building sites."
Peter Zeugin: "When a new house is being built in the countryside, Sunday walks still tend to lead to the construction site. One has a desire to know how people are going to live there later. When I built a house myself and later invited the

other residents of the village to come and see my new home, they had long been familiar with layout. They knew exactly where their new neighbors would sleep..."
Markus Zimmermann: *"Construction sites used to speak for themselves. Nowadays they are sealed off like maximum security wings. Our curiosity is just as great, but now we have to wait until the invitation to the 'construction-site event' arrives. And all the activities that such events involve – guided tours, info-points and glossy brochures – are often purely marketing instruments."*
Hans Conrad Daeniker: *"The charm of the arcane has gone and I'm not really interested in the marketing concept. You have to put on a helmet, allow yourself to be supervised by a neat assistant, and at the end you get sushi instead of grilled cervelat!"*

A hermetic barrier made of boards, a few barred peepholes that are too high for children, advertising posters and somewhere a sign offering a few bits of information about the project—this is the construction site as we know it. But a construction site begins much earlier. It begins in the minds of its neighbors, who are apprehensive about the noise, dirt and the dangers presented by construction-site traffic. The construction of a new building provokes legal protest from those whose view will be blocked and who fear increased traffic. Or it alarms the residents of a housing project scheduled for demolition, who want to know why they have to move out and where they should go.

Peter Zeugin: *"Boards and building commissions always assume that their members or clients are aware of what we have discussed in countless meetings. They do not understand that a professional process of communication is required."*

Construction sites are almost always a nuisance. And yet they also fascinate us and awaken our curiosity. Those commissioning construction projects today can and must utilize this ambivalence. Some of them are already doing this by providing "info boxes," constructing observation platforms and offering site tours. However, the zeal of investors in this respect flags quickly. As a rule they are satisfied when the building approval has been secured and they have found tenants or buyers for their building.

Peter Zeugin: *"Signing the building application is a tiresome obligation. And who still bothers with ground-breaking ceremonies? Yet these are two of many opportunities to keep buyers engaged who have pre-purchased their apartments. Then there is laying the foundation stone, the topping-out ceremony and first-time use. And why not even make the guarantee acceptance inspection after two years a formal, collective event?"*

Markus Zimmermann: *"Clients in both the private and cooperative sector automatically ask about the cost. They usually do not see the intellectual and long-term financial benefits of such 'staged events'."*

There are not many who think beyond the marketing aspect. And interestingly enough those who do represent the two extreme poles of the real-estate industry, i.e., noncommercial building clients and listed companies. Listed-company investors seek acceptance from shareholders, banks and evaluators. And noncommercial building clients, that is, cooperatives and the state, are accustomed to having to win the approval of their members or voters.

Learning from residential building cooperatives

The most experienced actors in this regard are building cooperatives involved in replacing their old building stock with new buildings. For this purpose they have to convince the residents involved (who are also their voting members!) to approve of radical changes. However, an investment in precise planning and long-term communication usually means a good chance of winning approval. Yet the struggle for acceptance often does not end with approval by the general meeting of housing cooperative members, whether because the decision disgruntles a minority, or because a majority or even consensus is required for a further stage or future projects.

Every construction site is associated with noise, dirt and odors. However, the construction phase is also a time of anticipation, and the moment of ground-breaking in the case of a new building is a cause for celebration. On the other hand, the start of a project in which a new building is replacing an old one means the demolition of established housing and the destruction of green areas and neighborhood structures. Many residents have to leave their homes against their will, and neighbors lose friends and acquaintances and perhaps fear that they, too, will soon be faced with the same situation. The onset of building work, in particular the start of demolition work, can therefore be an awkward moment. If this process is not carefully prepared and monitored, it can provoke resistance or strengthen resistance that has already developed. This situation can in turn put at risk further stages or other projects that rely on members' approval. The building cooperative can find itself paralyzed and the mood of its membership can enter a "downward spiral".

Based on such experiences, the "Förderstelle Gemeinnütziger Wohnungsbau", an advisory center affiliated with the Zurich section of the Swiss Housing Association (SVW), has developed a range of proposals for the organization of the communication process accompanying projects involving building replacement. Key recommendations include a well-planned concept for informing all affected parties and thoroughly organized building sites. Such measures should be designed to win acceptance within housing projects and neighborhoods and thus achieve two fundamental objectives:

1. The residential building cooperative positions itself as an innovative, prudent and exemplary project client that comprehensively informs all affected parties and takes all concerns seriously. In doing so, it creates the conditions for the necessary acceptance of subsequent project stages.
2. Members of the cooperative and interested neighborhood parties perceive the replacement building as an opportunity for beneficial development.

Due to the limited capacities of the cooperative board, administration and project planners, the implementation of many of the proposed measures is allocated to outside organizations. This is not merely expedient but also beneficial, since usually at this stage of a project architects, site managers and the client have quite different priorities. The general rule is, the earlier, the better. The earlier the developer looks into possible measures, systematically introduces them and provides targeted information about them, the lower the costs involved. In some circumstances the developer can even avoid delays due to legal actions if neighbors feel they are being taken seriously and are informed about concrete measures in good time. Many of the concrete measures recommended below can easily be integrated into the normal development of a project. Ongoing costs can be accommodated in the categories of "building site art" or "community support." In any case, the sustained benefits for the cooperative justify any costs accrued in this way.

Recommendations

Actively promoting the property or housing project as a historical location
The first stage involves the collection of documents and photographs. This can also entail the collection of oral histories from residents of the housing project or neighborhood. Housing records can be used to build up a "genealogy" of the residential area concerned. Who lived where at what time and where did these people move to later? This history of change can help to underpin the cooperative's own "transformation strategy".

The required research can be organized as a student project or as a project for retired members of the cooperative. It can include conversations with (former) residents as well as research in the cooperative and city archives. The information that is collected can be used as material for an exhibition (for example, in the new building), publications and media broadcasts.

Construction site and neighborhood

Commencement event: Replacing a building begins with a demolition. This is usually not regarded as grounds for celebration. For this reason a celebration or ritual marking the commencement of the project is staged prior to the beginning of demolition. This event includes not only residents and neighbors but also media, authorities and neighborhood organizations. → ILL.06.01

Temporary communal space adjoining the building site: The commencement event coincides with the opening of a temporary building that is a symbol of the new project. Located directly adjacent to the construction site and equipped with an observation platform on its roof, this building serves as a site for exhibitions and information events, and as a meeting place for both remaining and future residents. The design of the temporary building is the subject of a competition at the local college of design. → ILL.06.02 → ILL.06.03 Events during the construction process: An evening bar, a lunch canteen and/or a get-together for all concerned in the temporary communal building can help make the process of construction a positive experience. Occasional "consultation" sessions with the site management and the authorities promote trust. → ILL.06.04 → ILL.06.05

Website and webcam: The progress of construction can be observed at any time. The images are continually supplemented with important information about the project.

Construction sign: Rather than exhibiting the usual list of trades, the construction-site sign is used to provide project, schedule and contact information. Details of upcoming public neighborhood events can also be listed here.

Trucks, noise and dirt: The routes used by trucks are precisely defined and signposted. Rest periods during which trucks are not used are agreed on with the building firms and recorded in work contracts. Transport routes are regularly tidied up.

Safeguarding school routes: The safety of routes used by schoolchildren and intersections with transport routes is ensured through consultation with school authorities and police.

Guided tours: Senior school pupils are taken on site tours and provided with information on "construction site professions." Local residents and media representatives are invited to take part in tours.

Dismantling instead of demolishing

Housing cooperative projects are usually very well maintained. Given their good condition, proposed demolitions can meet with incomprehension. Pick-up day for present residents: On a certain date, perhaps in connection with a farewell party, residents are provided with expert help to remove any house

ILL.06.01
Taking leave: The former resident family posing in front of their small row house in the cooperative's courtyard garden, which has to make way for a replacement building.

ILL.06.02
Symbol of the new: The first structure to be erected on the site of the new Potsdamer Platz in Berlin was an "Info box," which itself cost several million euros to build. It served not only as an information center for visitors but also as a symbol of the new amidst the chaos of the Europe's largest construction site.

ILL. 06.03
The same can be achieved on a very small scale! Info-car, Architecture-Summer event, Dresden.

ILL.06.04
Art instead of vandalism: Rather than allowing the Werdwies housing project to be vandalized in the months leading up to demolition and thus creating problems for remaining tenants and the neighborhood, the Fuge cultural project was brought in to create artworks on the site in the intervening period.

ILL.06.05
Site huts are erected on the construction site of a Swiss general contractor to house a workshop and a canteen run by a qualified chef. The good working atmosphere generally benefits the area.

ILL.06.06
"A piece of Letzigrund": The legendary Letzigrund stadium is being replaced. Armed with carpet cutters and screwdrivers, around 1000 fans are entitled to take a piece of the pitch, chairs and cups home with them. An intelligent form of recycling.

ILL.06.07
Art on the construction site as part of the building process: The investor for the new Basel Trade Fair Tower financed a competition for temporary artworks on the construction site. It is also common practice for scaffolding to be used for lucrative poster advertising.

ILL.06.08
"Kunst am Bau" project for the Werdwies residential development, Zurich

ILL.06.09
Art on the construction site as part of the building process II: The group photo of the former residents will be displayed in an extremely large format in the stairwells of the replacement building. In this way the new residents are constantly reminded of the fact that other homes once stood on the site and other people lived here.

components and devices they want to take with them along with any plants they are particularly fond of. Before construction begins, building component exchanges and similar organizations are invited to come to the site and remove building components and devices under supervision.→ ILL.06.06

Communication
Building newspaper: A building newspaper reports on the progress of work, positive aspects, problems and their solutions, and any available jobs. It might also include articles on themes such as "Construction site professions" written in collaboration with firms working on the site. Circulation: To begin with, copies should be made available throughout the neighborhood and later twice a year for cooperative members and neighbors.

Consultation session: Once a month a carefully organized forum is held where concerns and problems can be tabled. The aim is not to provide immediate solutions but rather to have an open exchange and to discuss possible approaches. Interesting proposals are reported on in the building newspaper.

Letterbox: The building cooperative establishes a letterbox for direct questions, criticism and requests. This letterbox is regularly emptied and letters are answered promptly. Questions and answers of general interest are reported in the building newspaper.

Art on the construction site
Anyone who regards art on building sites as mere decoration runs the risk of missing an opportunity. Particularly in the case of replacement buildings art can itself become part of the process and forge a link between the old and the new. → ILL.06.07 → ILL.06.08

The modernization of a housing development that is organized in stages lends itself to events and rituals. Another possibility is a "memorial" that grows and changes together with the building—and thus establishes a connection with the history of the estate. → ILL.06.09 Appropriate ideas do not necessarily have to be developed in the context of a competition between artists or students. Another possibility is a supervised process involving the affected residents. Nostalgia for the old estate can be transformed into positive energy and exciting suggestions.

There is great potential and a range of possible starting points to cultivate acceptance of building projects and construction sites. The examples referred to here are intended as an illustration of proven ideas that can be used again and as a basis for further development.

CHAP. 08

THE PRIDE OF THE CONSTRUCTION SITE IS THE BUILDING SHELL

Friedrich Achleitner

If the city is comprehended as a construction site, then it follows that a construction site in the city is only a special case of normality. Everyone thinks they know what a construction site is, yet no one can describe where or how it begins and where or how it ends. Within the city a construction site is usually perceived as traffic congestion, as a congestion site. At yet the classic construction site is not static; it is a provocative kinetic phenomenon that is immovably fixed to a location. The life of the construction site consists in movement; everything moves towards a goal. The goal is the completed building, which exists as illusion. A stationary construction site is a premonition of disaster, a kind of reverse thrust. The state of a discontinued construction site is that of a ruin. The goal of the ruin is disappearance. Cynics and the politically bankrupt have invented the pathos of the ruin as value. All states leading to ultimate disappearance are perceived by the aesthete of the ruin as beautiful. Yet construction sites do not fit this schema because the construction site aesthetic was only invented in small fragments. Towering scaffolds can signify the conquest of space, future imaginings; they can awaken ideas but also mean withdrawal, disassembly, disappearance. The dismantling of a scaffold is a red-letter day for the space that the building occupies. The symbol of the construction site remains the scaffold. The scaffold is the first on the construction site and the last to leave. Interjection. A gentle yet insistent voice says to me: the symbol of the construction site is the crane. It controls the space above the construction site; it controls the location through its reach; it has access everywhere and the crane operator is the real emperor.

Admittedly: without the scaffolders (who assemble the scaffolds) nothing is possible. The crane controls the point, the scaffold the surface. Both are unafraid of heights.

The wind may blow through construction sites; puddles are allowed on construction sites. When one looks at the ground on building sites: mortar, sawdust, gravel, nails, synthetic materials, wire, paper, metal, plastic, box sections, slats, sheet metal, beams, stones, rubble; when one looks up, one stops. A construction site has holes. It is a world of transition, promise, the form of possibility. Every construction site has the atmosphere of a first day, the atmosphere of creation. The construction site knows no illusion; the construction site is a merciless place. A construction site is the truth unto itself. Good architectural critics love construction sites; bad architects avoid them. The construction site knows convention in terms of the production of illusion, not in terms of illusion itself. Construction sites are unpleasant contemporaries; they say only the truth. This truth lies in its reference to another truth. The truth of the construction site lies in its allusion to the truth of the completed building. The completed building alludes to the mendacity of social truths.

Construction sites are optimistic, forward-looking places; they are avow-edly positive, as long as the money doesn't run out. Construction sites are not only exterritorial but also humorless. The openness is only ostensible open-ness. Nothing is as precisely calculated as the future of a construction site, on a construction site. On the building site nothing is left to chance, and when chance enters the equation, it is an accident. The image of the construction site lives on the ignorance of the observer. One marvels at a construction site by looking into it. To begin with, construction sites are usually very deep, later they become progressively higher.

The pride of every construction site is the building shell. The building shell is a temporal marker; it designates the distance from building commencement to building completion. The building shell is a node within the process of construction. The building shell reveals as much of the future as the observer's imagination allows. The fascination of the building shell lies in its promise, its distance from the completed building. The building shell has no leeway but allows it to the observer, at least ostensibly. The completed building is the perfect disappointment. The completed building allows for nothing more. It is, after all, complete. Completed buildings that promise something else are architecture. Architecture is the promise of a building. The promise of the building shell cannot be trusted. The building shell is a revenant. If the building becomes derelict, the building shell appears again. And then it is just as talkative about the past as it was once imaginative about the future. Building shells are liars, although it is only they that reveal the truths of buildings. Building shells can be relied on. For this reason the building shell must be covered. Building shells are analogous to human beings—as long as they have a future.

ILL.08.01
Series by Andreas Muhs: Rohbau 1, 2, 3 and 4, Berlin, 1996

CHAP. 09

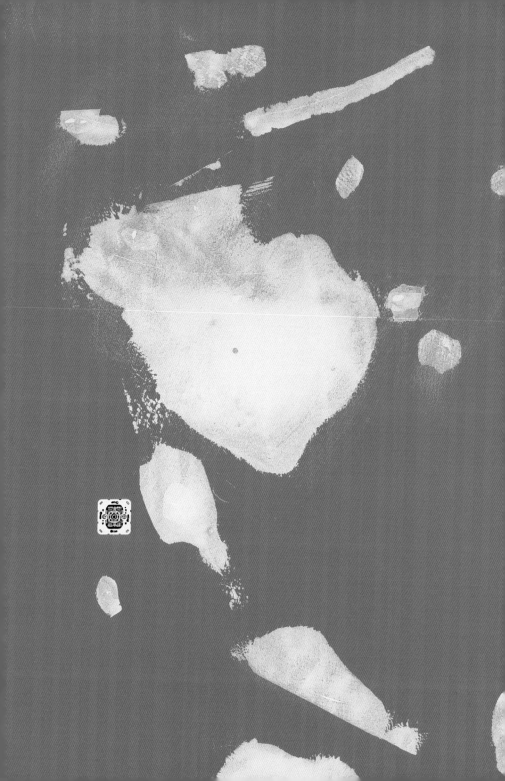

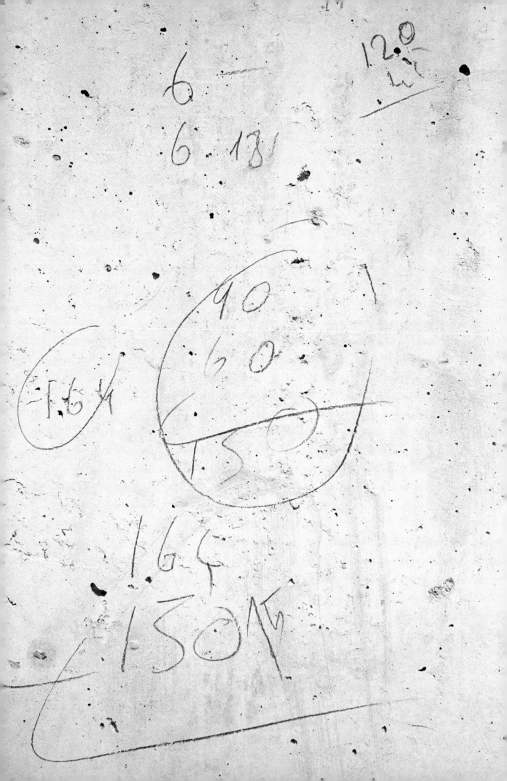

THE BEAUTY OF INCOM-PLETENESS

A BUILDING SITE?
THAT'S NOT ART!

Wilfried Dechau

Construction sites are dirty and chaotic. They reek of formwork oil and tar. German is sometimes only understood by the foreman; otherwise the mix of languages is positively Babylonian. And the form of address is anything but civilized. In summer the sun beats down relentlessly on your head or, even worse, on a barely ventilated hard hat. In winter everything is wet, the ground soft and muddy, and the moisture permeates your clothes. Or it is so bitterly cold that you would give anything to exchange your hard hat for a woolen pom-pom cap. Hardly cozy! And all this is supposed to have some aesthetic quality?

For those who don't like to get any rain spots on their Armani suits and prefer working in air-conditioned offices, who only have a vague sense of what has gone into a building project once it has been completed, who prefer a more cultivated form of address, in short, for those who prefer to engage with questions of art where it is warm and dry, the construction site offers little pleasure—at best what nuts, fools and enthusiasts capture there in pictures.

Indeed, one does need to be quite enthusiastic, a little foolish and just a wee bit mad to find something appealing in the dirty process of building. For such people the building site offers its own unique mix of characteristics.

How is it that someone who has been producing an architectural journal for over 20 years decides to spend time contemplating the beauty of incompleteness? Isn't that a contradiction? An architectural review is concerned least of all with incompleteness. Producing a journal for architects above all entails looking for the beauty of the complete project, and even more, being committed to it. It means always being in search of what is fresh, new and, if possible, not yet published. Photos of the (newly) completed building, which has of course not yet been marked by use, show readers, who are themselves mostly architects, what other architects have built. Legions of architectural photographers deliver material for this purpose. But woe betide the photographer whose picture reveals the slightest evidence that the paint might not yet even be dry. And any trace of the red and white plastic tape commonly used for cordons will cause editors to wrinkle up their noses. Although in the short time between "not completely new" and „already used" not a single blade of grass is allowed to grow, what the editor would really prefer is for everything to look (or be arranged) as if it has always been like this. On no account can the picture reveal traces of the construction process. This is captured only in photographs by foremen, site managers and building experts.

Yes, the question is justified: How does someone who has spent years producing journals and fixating on completeness come to turn his attention to incompleteness and even discover its peculiar beauty? In spite of (or because of) the fixations cultivated by my profession it has not escaped my attention that many buildings have long passed their zenith by the time they are completed. It is often the intermediate states of the construction process that seem worth recording. They exert a far greater fascination than the completed building, which often—smooth and waterproof—loses all the raw charm of the building shell. The photographer Andreas Muhs, for example, has photographed a whole series of concrete building shells, which in their honest nakedness have a graceful, buoyant and pure effect.→ **CHAP. 08, ILL. 08.01** However, my own experience has shown me how little of this charm remains once the gleaming "natural stone" covering has been applied. Indeed, it can even be the case that with completion everything becomes somehow reversed, opposite. I suspect that this is the reason why so little of what is built actually appears in architectural journals. One could continue this line of thinking and argue that what carpenters build is often (aesthetically) destroyed by roofers. The roof of a house is applied in the twinkling of an eye. The light, airy work of the carpenter, which subtly defines the space without yet abruptly and massively cutting it off, is henceforth hidden from view. Max Frisch's description of his own experience of this phenomenon is an apposite one: *"Now there is carpentry going on everywhere. The rafters have been laid and it looks*

ILL. 09.02
From a series by Dietmar Strauß

ILL. 09.04
Rhine bridge at Tamins

ILL. 09.06
Sabine Haubitz, Construction of the Pinakothek
der Moderne, ventilation shaft

*wonderful: the lattice of raw wood, the blue sky above it, for days on end the
clanging blows as they nail in formwork, wood shavings, sawdust, trucks
with new beams; it is unlikely that I will ever again have so much carpentry
around me; I am thoroughly enjoying it and walking around longer than
is necessary; it is what I like most about the whole process of building: the shell,
before the roofs are closed. Bricks and wood, rooms full of sky that can
be seen through all the stories; the cube has emerge for the first time but it
is transparent, and the space in which I am now standing is seeing the
sun for the last time, or at least the last time for decades. Over my head they*

are already working on the formwork, thrusting board against board." (Max Frisch, "Letzigraben, August 1948," Tagebuch 1946-1949, Frankfurt 1970 (1950), p. 210)

This phenomenon can be even more frustrating when office towers storm slowly upwards, story by story. Most of what were initially such auspicious, seemingly light and fragile building shells subsequently become cor-pulent, clumsy, disappointing. The incomplete has a particular, very transitory charm. The idea of recording it usually occurs to us too late or not at all. Yet copious photographs are taken of the finished, the final product—although it remains visible to everyone. The many stages of incom-pleteness, by contrast, can only be perceived over a limited, very brief period of time, after which the moments of unintended yet sometimes exotic charm are lost forever, become irretrievable—except in the a photograph. The freshly shuttered bridge → **ILL. 09.02** reveals its graphic charm to only a few and for only a short time. Soon the steel fixers arrive to create their equally transient artwork of reinforcing rods, which are soon concealed by the concrete mass that levels everything. Many a filigree scaffold exhibits an aesthetic quality at least on a par with that of the construction it contributes to. Yet once it has achieved its objective, it is carried away again—and can only be visual-ized in the photo. → **ILL. 09.04**

Without Lewis Wickes Hine's diligent documentation of the construction of the Empire State Building, our sense of how it was built would be a far more remote one. His extensive photographs fill whole books, and his work was commissioned by the project's clients. Sabine Haubitz, on the other hand, photographed the construction of the Pinakothek der Moderne → **ILL. 09.06** on her own initiative. Today, there are hardly any commissions for a stage-by-stage documentation of the building process. A comparison of pictures reveals what can be lost as a result. To be sure, a hiker in Switzerland's Graubünden region who comes across the wooden Traversinersteg suspension bridge will marvel at the fact that such an intricate design was created by engineers in such a remote mountain location. Admittedly, this alone is worth the trip. But how many of those who stop to catch their breath here and enjoy the view have an idea of how much more exciting the effect of this bridge was when it was in an almost complete yet still fragile state?

CHAP. 10

THE BUILDING SITE – WANDERING SOUND SOURCE OF THE CITY

Andres Bosshard

Listening to construction sites, comprehending the sonic swirls that press into the urban space in great waves—this is one of the tasks I have set myself as part of my research into urban sound. After encountering the ringing walls of the Indus Valley and witnessing the inner rhythm of complex arches supporting centuries-old vaults, I began to look at building in a quite different way. And when I heard the story of the wall-drummers in the Indian town of Uch, I decided to set out to track down the inner sound of the construction site.

"Hap!" "Dobrj, dobrj!" "Niej, ieh", "Ahhhhhlia..." Shouts echo through the courtyard of my building in Zurich; metallic blows resonate between the walls. "Finished tomorrow...!" The echo is so strong, I can barely understand the syllables. Over several minutes the rhythms accelerate, the shouts become more frequent, the blows more powerful, laughter, a large bar rolls across the asphalt, loud sliding noises, "zu zim fotografi," "metana, preta muta mmha dobrm..." The scaffolding has reached a new floor and workers

look through a window laughing. "Hehehe hahah isaa doia hoo hei potni potni hege!" It is only when the words have faded that I manage to discern a number of Serbian, Portuguese, Italian and now and again a few Swiss-German syllables. I'm just beginning to get used to the unfamiliar metal percussion outside, which is constantly interrupted by shouts from different heights, when a particularly loud yell tears me away from the work I had just begun. "Ehhh, porca miseria!" There is a sound of splitting wood, then two loud clangs, followed by the dull crack of a breaking windshield. About eight men climb down from the scaffolding and form a multilingual huddle around a car parked in the building courtyard that has a large scaffolding bar protruding from its front windshield.

Without immediately realizing it, I have been completely engrossed by the events outside my balcony window. Some weeks ago, batter boards were erected to mark out the dimensions of the building that is being constructed there—an obligatory practice here in Switzerland. At this time, the site is still empty and surrounded by a rough wooden fence. Weeds are growing thickly along the boundary, and several of the small, slightly rusting keep-out signs have already fallen onto the ground. Piles of gravel and sand ridged by truck tires lie around for no immediately apparent purpose. A few scraps of paper and plastic are blowing around in the wind. The site is empty and quiet, but all of us in the surrounding buildings know that any day now it will erupt into life. Even with our windows closed, our days will be filled with noise and the tea glass on my table will vibrate repeatedly as the huge pieces of construction machinery move back and forth. One morning the ground will be ripped open as if a nocturnal wave had swept away the topsoil. Behind large strips of plastic sheeting and a metal fence, loud noise, damp dust and mud will usher in the birth of a new building.

Some years ago I traveled through the Cholistan Desert. After a bumpy, dusty ride, I reached the town of Uch on the edge of the Indus Valley. Some way out of the town, whose magnificent old city gates adorned with faience could be seen glittering in the sun, the shrine to Princess Bibi Jawindi stood perched on a sand hill. → **ILLS.09.01, 09.02** My companions explained to me that the small sand hills dotting the land around the shrine were actually the remains of brickworks in which the bricks for the building had been fired and glazed. This remark led to me to conclude that all the colored walls and the cupolas that could be seen glowing mysteriously from a long way off had been made from materials that had been extracted from an area of desert around the building of less than one square kilometer.

In order to find the right place for a shrine, the old master builders first planted papyrus grass on a potential site. The way the plants grew showed

ILL.09.01, 09.02
Uchch, Pakistan:
The brick dome of the mausoleum in Bibi Jahwindi dates back to the thirteenth century. The building is one of the best preserved of the many domed mausoleums found in Uchch.

ILL.09.03
Queensboro Bridge, also known as the 59th Street Bridge, links Manhattan with Queens. The bridge was opened to traffic in 1909.

them how best to position the future building. The papyrus was then
harvested and made into charcoal pencils. Only these pencils could be used to
draw the plans for the building. I was also told that the construction of
the brickworks could only begin after clay pits had been located in the vicinity.
The size of the bricks was calculated to fit optimally into the hands of the
masons who had already been engaged. In addition, a number of experienced
drummers were employed to coordinate and direct the movements
of the masons all through the day. To my surprise I was told that these preparations meant stable walls could be built very quickly. And indeed,
the walls of the shrine, which were made of relatively small bricks, were very
thick and extremely precisely structured. I felt as if I could still hear the
driving drum beats as I attempted to follow the complex pattern in the cupolas.
The fan-like patterns repeated throughout the structure seemed like
the scores of a strange music that had been played into the walls at the time.
The shrine was crowned with dual-shell cupola that not only provided
optimal protection from the desert sun but could also convert the stored energy
to direct cool air from the ground into the shrine via intermediate chambers.
This passive air-conditioning system still functions perfectly today.

The three days I was able to spend in Uch were not enough for me to
collect all the information I wanted to about this building. However,
it became clear to me that the Bibi Jawindi Shrine had not been built like
an island in the desert. There had been a whole network of such
buildings spread over the desert at regular intervals. The cities in the region
had also been planned and constructed to function as energy networks.
The resonance of the sound in the buildings and their courtyards was not only
a self-evident feature of the cities but was planned from the beginning
and carefully structured during the building process.

The courtyard below my balcony is suddenly quiet. It's obviously lunchtime. Since the majority of workers on construction sites can take
their lunch break at the same time, the level of noise in the whole city drops
for a time. On average, seven small or large construction sites are located
within each square kilometer. They spew out sound like sonic volcanoes, feeding
it into the vibrating urban space. Are the master builders, architects
and site managers aware of its existence? Or are there among today's skilled
laborers perhaps direct descendants of the medieval freemasons who
today wear white overalls and ear muffs and work with hydraulic tools on open
building platforms? The powerful rhythms of pile drivers fly over the
river, feeding unexpectedly on the vibrations of the old railway bridge brought
to maximum-volume life for three minutes 30 times a day by a 100 m long
tanker train.

In 1932, Edgard Varèse carefully noted down the interlocking cascades of sound coming from one of the largest construction sites of the time. He stood on the East River in New York where the Queensboro Bridge now stands → ILL.09.03 and listened to the city of New York. His revolutionary composition not only explored the tonal colors of sirens and the percussive rhythms of everyday life, but also their expressive movements in space. "…the feeling of being catapulted into the space with the help of sources of sound at numerous points (in the space). By counter-rhythms that do not refer to one another but are simultaneously played out," was the way he described the sensation that informed his composition Amérique, which premiered in Philadelphia in 1932. Varèse's research into sound spaces reached its highpoint at the 1958 World's Fair in Brussels, where he created the "Polytop" Pavilion together with Le Corbusier and Jannis Xenakis. → ILL.09.04

The pavilion's sonic architecture made it possible for a large audience to "step inside" the music and experience the movement of sounds. This change in spatial perspective is fundamental. The music opened up a sonic construction site that today is still only in its beginning stages.

In 1980, Bill and Mary Buchen erected a large wind harp at the counterpoint to the sound ellipse that encloses the Queensboro Bridge in New York. The wind harp was positioned in the center of an empty site on the opposite side of the East River, surrounded by semi-dilapidated floating docks. The area was being used by a group of artists from Long Island as a sculpture-construction site known as "Socrates Park". In the midst of the drone of the city sounds, a refined, buzzing voice could suddenly be heard. Vibrated by irregular gusts of wind, dozens of carefully tuned steel strings emitted a strange, electroniclike mix of sound towards a satellite dish swaying 12 m above the ground on the mast of a sailing ship. Nearby the windharp mast, the whirring crescendos of helicopters amalgamated acoustically with the deep, echoing beats of car tires on the bridge some 300 m away. A swirling acoustic space was created that came and went with each gust of wind. Together with the gentle rise and fall of the sonic clusters emitted by the steel strings, the sonic space emerged over and over from the city noise, only to disappear again into the acoustic flood. A listener prepared to spend at least 20 minutes here would gradually become aware of resonance fields that remained suspended in the space when the wind dropped. The tones of the wind harp initiated a process of sonic transformation. The acoustic flood divided and began to take on a new voice independent of the source of sound. The catalytic string sounds, as fine as they were, exerted an unfamiliar, almost uncanny power. First they took hold of the raw urban sonic wind and changed its frequencies. Then they forced the newly

ILL.09.04
Philips Pavilion at the World's Fair,
Le Corbusier und Jannis Xenakis, Brussels 1958

colored sounds onto different spatial tracks and allowed new intermediate
spatial zones to emerge from the swirling channels. Sound generated
space. In the Socrates Park, the sculptural building site became a regenerator
of urban sound, at least within the range of the wind harp's sound. The
sonic architects Mary and Bill Buchen understood how. Based on their experiences in the Socrates Park, they have planned and built other wind-sound
parks. The Socrates Park construction site, like all construction sites, was only
temporary. The phenomena of sound transformation became progressively
weaker and finally disappeared completely. Even the fleeting memories of them
retained for a time by the former visitors to the old harbor on the East
River ultimately faded. The noise of the city closed the sound space over and
flooded the now no longer empty Socrates Park site.

Every construction site holds hidden energies in its invisible core, where space emerges within space, where raw, uninhabitable space becomes inhabitable space. The transformation of the urban space by every construction space seems to us to happen in a fleeting moment. "Construction site" is synonymous with a state of emergency which is particularly difficult to comprehend when observed from outside. The epicenters of the contemporary complex urban organism are constituted by construction sites that move around, and yet they are one of the fundamental sources of the permanent cityscape. The construction site of the "Ile Seguin-Rives de Seine" development of a new cultural quarter on the former site of the Renault factory in Paris illustrates how a process of urban transformation can be staged in the contemporary context. The Intégral Ruedi Baur et Associés design agency has developed a comprehensive communication system for the large-scale construction site in the former industrial part of the city. It allows the gigantic construction site to be read as an urban orchestration that one can experience throughout the whole of its transformation. The enormous pieces of script, which, as it were, seem to interpose themselves into the building process, make the entire construction area into an urban stage that serves as a nonstop presentation of its own emergence.

While the art actions on the gigantic construction site in Berlin's Mitte district were designed as selective interventions and captured moments in the process of transition, here in Paris the process is being staged as an urban musical score. Although in Berlin the city's symphony orchestra performed Beethoven's Fifth to a ballet of construction cranes, the internal acoustics and sound of the space were not taken up as a theme. For a short time, the construction site became a public arena in which a contiguity and confusion of urban events could be played out.

The micro- and macroscopic spatial dimensions that are set in vibration on every building site hold a secret not yet revealed. How can the sound of permanently active construction sites be shaped? The construction site offers the potential to be acoustically orchestrated in the same way the "Ile Seguin-Rives de Seine" project has been visually shaped. The musical vision and the media and instruments for its realization are ready and waiting.

BIOGRAPHIES

Friedrich Achleitner is an architectural critic and journalist. He studied architecture with Clemens Holzmeister and until 1958 worked as a freelance architect, then as a freelance writer (member of the "Vienna Group") and a university lecturer. Prior to being awarded emeritus status in 1998, he was director of the department of "History and Theory of Architecture" at the University of Applied Arts Vienna. He has written numerous literary works, including and or or and (2006), as well as works on architecture, including Austrian Architecture in the 20th Century (1980-95).

Margrit Bion is an architect who works in a range of capacities, including from her own office in Zurich and for Skidmore Owings & Merill (SOM) in New York. She is certified as an international project manager (IPME), and since 1996 has been the managing director of Steiner (Deutschland) GmbH, a subsidiary of Karl Steiner AG. She supervises large-scale projects in Germany, from planning through to construction, and has worked as a project manager/controller for Karl Steiner AG in China and Thailand.

Andres Bosshard is a freelance musician, composer and sound artist. After studying music (flute) and art history in Zurich, he initially devoted himself to painting and a series of performance actions before turning to experimental music. Since 1995 he has undertaken extensive trips to India, Pakistan and Japan. In 2002 he was the artistic director of the "Klangturm" at the Swiss Expo.02 national exhibition in Biel. Since 2000 he has collaborated with architects and landscape architects on several ongoing sound-architecture projects. In 2003 he was a guest professor at the Academy of Media Arts in Cologne, and in 2006 he was a lecturer at the Zurich University of Design and Arts.

Beat Büchler is an economist. After completing her studies, she worked in marketing for a large construction firm. Since 1995 she has been managing director of the Swiss General Contractors Association (VSGU) and the Swiss Building Industry Group (SBI). Her work involves representing the interests of large building firms and general contractors.

Hans Conrad Daeniker is a freelance consultant for internal and external communications, particularly for cooperative societies, associations and foundations. He studied economic and social history and political science

→ **Peter von Holzen**
photography by Christian Schwager,
Winterthur

→ **Jana Gunstheimer**
With the kind permission of
Galerie Conrads, Düsseldorf and
Galerie Römerapotheke, Zurich

→ **Felix Schramm**
With the kind permission of
ausstellungsraum25, Zurich
photography by Martin Stollenwerk,
Zurich

→ **Miklos Gaál**
architekturbild 2005
© Miklos Gaál, Helsinki

→ **Marcel Gähler**
with the kind permission of
Galerie Römerapotheke, Zurich

→ **Kerim Seiler**
© 2007 ProLitteris, Zurich,
photography: Kerim Seiler

→ **Marcus Buck**
architekturbild 2003
© Marcus Buck, Munich

→ **Taiyo Onorato & Nico Krebs**

→ **Gabriela Gerber und
Lukas Bardill**
© 2007 ProLitteris, Zurich
With the kind permission of
Galerie Luciano Fasciati, Chur
and Galerie staubkohler Zurich
photography: Gabriela Gerber and
Lukas Bardill

→ **Lutz & Guggisberg**
© 2007 ProLitteris, Zurich
With the kind permission of
Anna Helwing Gallery, Los Angeles

→ **Ingo Giezendanner (GRRRR)**
© 2007 ProLitteris, Zurich

→ **Dieter Leistner**
© Dieter Leistner, Würzburg

→ **Judit Villiger**
with the kind permission of Galerie
Römerapotheke, Zurich.
Annotation: La friche = wasteland
Château rouge = Part of the Goutte d'Or
district in the North of Paris
Zurich 4 – Paris 18 = A cultural
exchange between two comparable
urban neighbour hoods in which seven
artists from Zurich were invited to Paris
and vice versa

→ **Stefan Schilling**
architekturbild 2005
© Stefan Schilling, Cologne

→ **Cat Toung**
photography by Cat Toung

In recent years the concept of the "construction site" has become established as a symbol of upheaval and emergence, a motto for change and a metaphor for the processual. The phenomenon of the construction site has latent relevance as a theme within contemporary art: whether in terms of an actual representation of the construction site as pictorial motif or a symbolization of the changeable character of the construction site, which the artwork expresses as precariousness and provisionality.

The construction site as a locus of occurrence and genesis also provides an analogy for the process of artistic production and the studio as locus of the genesis of art. The Dadaist Kurt Schwitters' "Merzbau" is an exemplary illustration of this. His giant, traversable sculpture – a convoluted and constructed interior space filled with a huge variety of materials and found objects that evokes associations with both sacred architecture and cavelike spaces – was the product of 30 years of work undertaken by Schwitters in the early part of the 20th century, work which was never completed. The principle of incompleteness is programmatic; work as process rather than the completed artwork is the focus of the work. The concept of incompleteness and the processual has fundamentally altered our understanding not only of art but also the concept of the work, as indicated by the prevalence in recent art history of the terms "open artwork"[1] and "work in progress."

In contemporary art, the dialogic process between the genesis of a work and the self-conception of the artist presents itself as an eternal construction site in the prosaic sense. Today's artist is usually an architect, structural engineer, planner, building laborer and site manager all rolled into one. Every anticipated work is a potential construction site, every discarded one a building stoppage, every completed one a construct of ideas that has been given material form. Artistic practice, the artist's biography, is itself a work in progress, a construction site that holds within it a promise of the future. Life, art – a construction site.

Silvia Lorenz

---

[1] In 1962 Umberto Eco published "The open artwork," one of the most influential works in the field of modern aesthetics, in which he established "openness" as a central criterion of modern art. Openness in this context refers to the fact that an artwork does not transport an unambiguous meaning that is predetermined by the artist. Rather, the recipient plays a significant role in the creation of the artwork in that he or she interprets the work and attributes an individual meaning to it.

INCOMPLE-
TENESS AS
ARTISTIC
CONCEPT

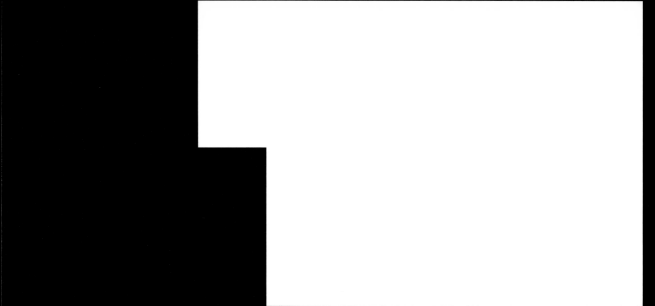

and has worked as a journalist (most recently for Swiss Television) and party secretary, as well as completing further training in the areas of process support and organization development. Since 1996 he has been a member of the AmGleis Gmbh office partnership. He is an information officer for the Zurich section of the Swiss Housing Federation (SVW), a representative for the Wohnbund network and vice-president of a mid-sized cooperative society.

Wilfried Dechau is an author and photographer. He initially studied architecture and was engaged as an assistant lecturer in the field of structural design and industrial construction in Braunschweig; 1980–1988, editor of the Deutsche Bauzeitung (db); 1988–2004, editor-in-chief of the db; 1995–2001, teaching positions at the Biberach University of Applied Science; and since 1999, member of the Deutsche Gesellschaft für Photographie (DGPh). In 1995 he initiated the European architectural photography prize "architekturbild," which led to the founding of the non-profit organization "architekturbild e.v." in 2003. Since 2004 he has been a member of the advisory board of the Bauhaus Foundation Dessau.

Dietmar Eberle is an architect who studied at the Vienna Technical University. In 1979 he was a co-founder of the building-artist movement in Voralberg. Since 1979 he has collaborated and shared an office with Carlo Baumschlager; since 1983, teaching positions in Hanover, Vienna, Linz, Zurich, New York and Darmstadt; since 2001, professor of architecture at the Swiss Federal Institute of Technology (ETH) Zurich and director of the ETH Wohnforum–Centre for Cultural Studies in Architecture; 2003–2005, dean of the ETH Faculty of Architecture.

Marie Antoinette Glaser is a cultural anthropologist; studied literature and ethnology; 1999–2004, visiting lecturer at the Institute for Interdisciplinary Research and Continuing Education (IFF) at the University of Vienna; organizational responsibility for the "Integrated Studies" interdisciplinary seminar held at the IFF in conjunction with the city of Vienna; since 2004, academic project manager at the ETH Wohnforum–Centre for Cultural Studies in Architecture; since 2007, visiting lecturer at the ETH Faculty of Architecture, "Wohnen / Habitation" lecture series. Her research focuses on interdisciplinary research of residential culture, history of daily life and culture, the city and perception.

Anna Joss has been an assistant lecturer at the ETH Wohnforum–Centre for Cultural Studies in Architecture since 2007, with her research focusing on house biographies, building, residential and urban history; studied history, modern German literature and art history at the University of Zurich; worked as an undergraduate teaching assistant in the Department of Social Studies of Science at ETH Zurich (2005–2006) and at the Institute for Cultural Studies in Art, Media and Design (ICS) at the Zurich University of Design and Arts (2004–2006).

Peter Kaufmann is an architect with the firm of Baumschlager & Eberle in Lochau (A); attended art school in Zurich, studied architecture at ETH Zurich and at the Harvard GSD/USA; worked for three years in Holland; diverse publications; currently teaches under Dietmar Eberle at ETH Zurich.

Mikael Krogerus has been the editor of NZZ Folio since 2005; studied political science at the Free University Berlin and completed his studies at the Kaospilot University in Aarhus/Denmark, following study visits to Durban and New York; during his studies, worked as a copywriter for different advertising agencies and as an editor for the young people's TV program Chat the Planet in New York.

Silvia Lorenz studied fine arts and since 2002 has worked as an art and culture facilitator in a range of contexts (documenta11, MDR, Swiss National Museum, Theaterhaus Gessnerallee). Since 2003 she has also been an art dealer. From 2006–2007, assistant lecturer at the Institute for Theory at the Zurich University of Design and Arts.

Sacha Menz has been a professor of architecture and building processes at ETH Zurich since 2004; 1990, founded the architectural firm Sacha Menz und Kuno Schumacher in Zurich; 1991, founded the Joran Sport AG in Zurich and Taiwan, which specialized in the production and construction of bicycles; since 1997, co-partner with Dolf Schnebli and Tobias Ammann in the architectural firm of sam architekten und partner ag (since 2005, schnebli menz sam architekten und partner ag), based in Zurich and Verscio; since 2001, a member of various architectural juries; since 2002, permanent member of the architectural advisory committee to the city of Ostfildern; since 2005, president of the Zurich section of the SIA (Swiss engineering and architectural association) and member of the BSA (Federation of Swiss Architects).

Paul Meyer is an architect and the author of *Gesamtleitung von Bauten* (*Construction Management*) 2003, a standard work in Swiss architectural colleges and in the field of building project management; 1968–1973, project and business manager with the Metron planning firm; 1973–1987, University Master Builder for the canton of Zurich, subsequently professor of building realisation at ETH Zurich.

Markus Zimmermann is an architect; following 20 years working in planning and as a member of the board of the Bauplan architectural cooperative, since 2000 he has been the director of the Förderstelle Gemeinnütziger Wohnungsbau, an advice center run collectively by the Zurich section of the Swiss Housing Association (SVW) and the city of Zurich.

LIEBHERR

STEINER
TOTAL SERVICES CONTRACTOR

Implenia®

feldmann
Bauunternehmung
Bilten + Jona

sihlc|ty
vertreten durch Credit Suisse
und Swiss Prime Site AG

mch
messe schweiz
marketing live.

c' r' b'

KIBAG

KIBAG. Aus gutem Grund.

Alfred Müller AG

SBV
SSE
SSIC
Schweizerischer Baumeisterverband
Société Suisse des Entrepreneurs
Società Svizzera degli Impresari-Costruttori
Societad Svizra dals Impressaris-Constructurs

ACKNOWLEDGEMENTS

Sincere thanks to:
Anna Joss for her tireless engagement, Dietmar Eberle, Kristian Koch, Hans-Martin Frech, Adrian Lehmann, Ulrich Widmer, Martin Fehle, Felix Schmid, Hans-Peter Domanig, Conradin Stiffler, Herbert Oberholzer, Heinz Ruettimann, Ferdinand Zoller, David Spiess, Andreas Gnädinger, Wilfried Dechau, Rebecca Zuber, Reto Winkelmann, Nicolas Häberli, Lars Müller, Katharina Kulke, Silvia Lorenz, Peter Kaufmann, Klaus Spechtenhauser, Andreas Huber, Michelle Corrodi, Inge Glaser, Susanne Gysi, Christopher Latkoczy and all those who have contributed to the successful completion of this book.
For Linus, who came into the world in April.

We would like to thank the following sponsors for their generous support:
Liebherr International Deutschland GmbH (Main sponsor), Implenia, CRB Schweizerische Zentralstelle für Baurationalisierung, Feldmann Bau AG, KIBAG, Alfred Müller AG, SBV Schweizer Baumeisterverband, Sihlcity represented by Credit Suisse and Swiss Prime Site AG, Karl Steiner AG, Messe Schweiz.

PHOTOGRAPHIC CREDITS

Airbus S.A.S. 2007
→ 25 r
akg-images, Erich Lessing
→ 13, 14 l
Photo Basilisk
→ 112 t r
Bettmann / CORBIS
→ 130 b
BMW Group
→ 25 t r
Marcus Buck
→ 68, 69, 70 t l–70 b l, 70 b r, 71
Markus Dlouhy
→ 55, 56, 61, 62, 76–81, 82 b l, 83–99
Wilfried Dechau
→ 124 o r
Michele Falzone / JAI / Corbis
→ 130 t r, 130 t l
Frick Byers / Getty Images
→ 29 t r
Christian Gerber
→ 111 b r
Marie Antoinette Glaser
→ 18 l
Maurice Grünig
→ 111 t l, 112 b l
Samuel Haettenschweiler
→ 111 b l
Sabine Haubitz
→ 124 b
Rahel Hegnauer
→ 112 b l
Jörg Hempel
→ 111 t c
Ron Herron, Archigram
→ 29 b
Implenia Generalunternehmung AG
→ 82 t l, 82 c l, 82 t r, 82 c r
In nome dell'architettura,
Angelo Mangiarotti, 1987
→ 29 t l
Andreas Muhs
→ 119

Liebherr-Werk Biberach GmbH
→ 70 t r, 72, 73, 74 b r
Miteigentümerschaft Sihlcity, Zürich
→ 100, 101, 102, 103
Photography Collection,
Miriam & Ira D. Wallach Division of Art Prints,
and Photographs, The New York Public Library,
Astor, Lenox and Tilden Foundations
→ 18 r
picture-alliance / dpa
→ 23 l
picture-alliance / Godong
→ 23 r
PR, architektursommer-dd.de, C. Berger
→ 11 t r
Dietmar Strauß
→ 124 t l
Studio Monte Rosa, Prof. Andrea Deplazes, D-ARCH, ETHZ, 2006
→ 25 l
Michael S. Yamashita / CORBIS
→ 14 r
Stadt Zürich
→ 112 t r

ProLitteris 2007 Zurich Fernand Léger

© Lars Müller Publishers 2008

Idea and concept: Marie Antoinette Glaser
Coordination and assistance: Anna Joss

Design concept and layout;
Idea and concept artwort sequence:
Nicolas Haeberli, www.buerohaeberli.ch
Reto Winkelmann, www.retowinkelmann.ch

Artwork selection: Silvia Lorenz;
Wilfried Dechau

Translation: Joe O'Donnell
Proofreading: John O'Toole
Production: Marion Plassmann

Printing: Konkordia GmbH
Binding: Josef Spinner Buchbinderei GmbH

Typography: Morgan Avec
Paper: Munken Print White, Mega Gloss

Lars Müller Publishers
5400 Baden/Switzerland
www.lars-mueller-publishers.com

Printed in Germany
ISBN 978-3-03778-112-8
ISBN 978-3-03778-111-1 (German)